W9-BDR-990

Presented to

_____

By

_____

On the Occasion of

_____

Date

_____

A HEART FOR PRAYER

Encouragement for Your Prayer Life

GERT MCINTOSH

BARBOUR
PUBLISHING

Published by Barbour Publishing, Inc., P.O. Box 719,
Uhrichsville, Ohio 44683 www.barbourbooks.com

*Our mission is to publish and distribute inspirational products
offering exceptional value and biblical encouragement to the
masses.*

ecpa Member of the
Evangelical Christian
Publishers Association

Printed in the United States of America.

5 4 3 2 1

DEDICATION

In memory of my beloved husband, Harold,
who for fifty-three years was not only
everything a good husband should be
but also a praying Christian.

INTRODUCTION:
THE GIFT OF PRAYER

The gift of prayer accompanies the gift of salvation. As unbelievers, we are cut off from God, but when we accept and welcome Jesus Christ into our hearts and lives, we are given a direct line of communication with Him.

He gives each of us different gifts to be used for Him, but the most powerful and delightful gift to every Christian is the gift of prayer. God wants us to confess and ask and praise and place our needs before him. That's how we grow "near to the heart of God."

The almighty Creator of the universe desires our fellowship! We must never take this amazing gift for granted, but rather study God's Word to learn how He wants us to pray.

My prayer life has not been (and is not) always what it should be—but in the many years since I placed my faith in Jesus Christ it has grown stronger and sweeter as I seek to pray God's way. I have experienced thousands of answers to prayer, and I have seen God answer countless prayers in the lives of others, solving their problems and meeting their needs.

My hope is that this book will bring to your mind

and heart the things God has said about prayer, and you will develop a strong, dependent, and delightful relationship with Him by praying His way. Experience the awesome ways He will work when you bow your heart, your mind, and your life to Him with a true heart for prayer!

THE MOST IMPORTANT
PRAYER OF YOUR LIFE

*For whosoever shall call upon
the name of the Lord shall be saved.*

ROMANS 10:13

The first and foremost requirement of having a true heart for prayer is to pray the most important prayer of your life, the prayer of repentance for God to save you through Jesus Christ. Until we pray this prayer of repentance, we have no connection to God and we have no right to ask Him for anything because we are not His children. Jesus said, "Not every one that saith unto me, Lord, Lord, shall enter into the kingdom of heaven; but he that doeth the will of my Father which is in heaven" (Matthew 7:21). And the will of God is for us to believe in Jesus and have eternal life with Him.

Have you prayed this most important prayer in order to be saved? If you have not, you can do so now. You simply must believe that you are a sinner and confess your sin to God. Believe that Jesus Christ died on a cross, shedding His blood to forgive your sins, and rose again to conquer death, giving you the hope of eternal life with Him. Then ask Jesus to come into your heart and life and help you to live for Him.

If you have already prayed the most important prayer of your life, you know how, when, and where it happened. You remember what caused you to pray it. It was the day your life changed forever as you became a child of God! Our pastor recently asked every person in our church to write down his or her testimony. It is a great blessing to read the testimonies of individuals as they recount how they met God face to face one day and their lives were changed forever.

One of the most powerful testimonies in the Bible is the conversion of the Apostle Paul in Acts 9. Paul's life is proof that no sin is too great to be washed away by the precious blood of Jesus Christ. Paul was a persecutor and murderer of Christians until God met him on the road to Damascus and called him to be His child. From then on, Paul was no longer an enemy of the followers of Jesus. Instead, he gave his heart and life to God to use him in order to preach the gospel of Jesus Christ to all people.

Paul's life is an awesome example of what God can do in us if we give our hearts and lives to Him. When we come to Him to be saved, we find our true purpose in life, the very reason He created us—to have fellowship with Him!

ALIVE IN CHRIST

Likewise reckon ye also yourselves
to be dead indeed unto sin,
but alive unto God through Jesus Christ our Lord.

ROMANS 6:11

Yield yourselves unto God,
as those that are alive from the dead.

ROMANS 6:13

I knew a woman who went daily for years to her husband's grave to talk to him. I know she wasn't receiving any answers. She was talking to him not with him. Do we talk to God or with Him? Only if we are alive to Him can we carry on a real conversation, and it is abundantly evident in His Word that there is no other way to be alive to God except through Jesus Christ.

There is nothing going on between God and sinners. They are dead to Him. They have no real regard for Him, nor have they ever tried to get to know Him. They may try to pray from time to time, but it is like conversing with a dead person. There is no connection, and there will never be any answer. They depend on themselves instead of God.

There is little going on between God and those who call themselves Christians but have not submitted their lives to Christ. They may pray a few lukewarm prayers or seek Him out in time of need, but there is no living, vital, everyday relationship with Him. Perhaps they talk to God but never listen to His side of the conversation through His Word.

There is much going on between God and those who have put their trust in Him through Jesus Christ. There is love and fellowship and dependence on Him. They pray, and God answers. They do not pray just to get answers but because they want to have fellowship with Him, and this is the perfect fulfillment of the creation of man.

When we accept Jesus Christ as our Savior, He literally brings us out of the inevitable, eternal death of sin so that one day we will have eternal life with Him. And in the meantime, we can be alive not only physically, but also spiritually—living, loving, and communicating with God exactly as He intended!

WHAT PRAYER DOES FOR YOU

The following are some of the wonderful ways I have experienced the power of prayer in my life, and I hope you will experience them, too!

PRAYER:

- Bonds your soul to others in a unique way whether you are praying for someone or with someone, and it bonds your soul to God through Christ.
- Gives you a rare quiet time in the day. God knows we need to come apart with Him before we totally come apart!
- Gives you great peace of mind and soul, which is probably the most amazing thing about prayer. It is hard to explain but easy to experience if you are willing to try.
- Gives you much hope and joy.
- Gives you the patience you need daily with your children, your spouse, your family, your friends, and your coworkers.
- Gives you victory in Jesus! This is the theme song of the church I attend (and probably of

many churches). We sing it heartily on Sunday mornings because it speaks of living victoriously through the circumstances of the past week and hope for more victories the next week.

- Helps you overcome weakness and resist temptation.
- Helps you realize how much God loves you. We read over and over in God's Word of His love for us in spite of our weakness and failures. When we pray, we experience that love.
- Makes you aware of the needs of others and helps you love them.
- Relieves your fears. If God is for us, who can be against us?
- Turns your eyes upon Jesus. You experience the presence of God and know you are pleasing Him. This is true worship!

ANSWERS TO PRAYER

When we pray, meeting God's conditions and believing His promises, we can fully expect God to answer. We must understand, however, that His answers are not necessarily always what we want or expect them to be. Sometimes we tell God exactly what we think we need, but He has something better for us. God answers prayer in four different ways:

Immediately. When Peter attempted to walk on the water and began to sink because of His doubts, he called on Jesus to save Him. Even though Jesus chided him for his lack of faith, He answered Peter's prayer immediately.

Delayed. When Jesus raised Lazarus from the dead, He waited a couple days after he heard Lazarus was sick before He went to him. When He arrived there, Lazarus's sister, Martha, accused Him of not caring. She said, "Lord, if thou hadst been here, my brother had not died" (John 11:21). At the same time, she told him she had complete faith that whatever He asked of God would be done immediately. She didn't realize it was necessary to wait until there was no doubt about

Lazarus being dead before Jesus brought him back to life in order to bring greater glory to God.

No. Paul asked God three times to remove his thorn in the flesh but realized that it kept him humble and looking to God. God's grace gave him victory over his aggravating, ever-present weakness or disability. He said he could take pleasure in anything he had to endure for Christ's sake because it made him depend on God more and himself less. God's grace was sufficient for Paul, and it is for you and me. We do, indeed, learn the grace of God through delayed or unanswered prayer.

Another way. God's ways are above our ways, and we don't know what His perfect will is for us; but we must be willing to accept a totally different answer than what we may have envisioned. When Elisha told Naaman to dip in the Jordan River seven times to heal his leprosy, Naaman was angry and didn't want to do such a simple, foolish thing. At his servant's urging, however, he did it, and God completely healed him. And Naaman glorified God!

Ask God for grace to receive His answer whatever it may be.

A DELAYED ANSWER

Lord, behold, he whom thou lovest is sick.

JOHN 11:3

What a simple prayer! Mary and Martha simply sent a message to their friend, Jesus, that Lazarus was sick. Of course Jesus knew that Lazarus was sick, but He was waiting for them to call on Him even as He is waiting for us to call on Him for help.

Mary and Martha learned that God does not always work the way we think He will or should. It seemed that Jesus should have come right away when He heard about Lazarus, but instead he waited for two days. Often, like Martha, we become anxious and begin to think God doesn't care about us when He delays in answering our prayers. This is where real faith comes in—faith that God will accomplish the best for us according to His perfect will and timing. Learning to wait on God is an extremely important part of our prayer life.

Before His miraculous answer to the prayer for Lazarus, Jesus led Martha to confess her belief in Him and His power. His question in John 11:26 was, "And whosoever liveth and believeth in me shall never die.

Believest thou this?" Martha confessed that Jesus was the Messiah, the Son of God who came into the world, the Resurrection and the Life, and called Him Lord! We must believe the absolute reality of these things as well or else He cannot and will not answer our prayers.

In John 11:35, "Jesus wept." When they led Jesus to where Lazarus lay dead, He wept; and the onlookers said, "Behold how he loved him!" We must remember that Jesus loves us with an everlasting love and wants to answer our prayers and meet our needs.

How many times have we looked back and thanked God that He did not answer our prayer immediately or according to our expectations? As in this case with the prayer for Lazarus, Jesus had something much better in mind, something that exceeded all their dreams, expectations, or understanding. They believed that Jesus could have healed Lazarus if He had come sooner, but He had waited too long and Lazarus was dead. Could Jesus raise him from the dead? That had never even entered their minds!

Eye hath not seen, nor ear heard,
neither have entered into the heart of man,
the things which God hath prepared
for them that love him.

1 CORINTHIANS 2:9

WHEN GOD SAID "NO" TO PAUL

There was given to me a thorn in the flesh. . . .
For this thing I besought the Lord thrice,
that it might depart from me.

2 CORINTHIANS 12:7–8

No one knows what Paul's thorn in the flesh was, although many have tried to guess or profess to know. Surely that was the design of God, so that no matter what our particular trouble or problem is, we can relate to what Paul said about it. We know that it was something that 1) was personal, 2) came from Satan and was permitted by God, 3) he struggled with, 4) kept him humble, and 5) he prayed three times to have removed.

If anyone should have a prayer answered, surely it was the apostle Paul. He left his life of honor and prestige and respect the day he met Christ on the road to Damascus. Later, he was beaten, stoned, and shipwrecked. He made long missionary journeys; traveled through unsafe countries; suffered the dangers of city and wilderness; experienced pain, hunger, and thirst; and was often cold and without proper clothing—all to preach and teach the gospel of Jesus Christ!

Three times Paul asked for relief from his vexing problem. He received an answer the third time he asked. God said, "My grace is sufficient for thee: for my strength is made perfect in weakness" (2 Corinthians 12:9). This answer satisfied Paul, and he stopped asking God to take away his infirmity because he realized his faith would be made stronger by drawing on God's grace to live each day. His grace is sufficient for our every need, too, if we let Him control our daily walk. Sometimes God needs our weaknesses more than He needs our strength, for it is then that He is glorified.

God often shows us that the best answer to our prayers is not to take us out of our trials but to give us His strength to live gracefully through them.

WHY GOD ANSWERED "NO" TO JESUS' PRAYER

And he went a little farther, and fell on his face,
and prayed, saying, O my Father, if it be possible,
let this cup pass from me: nevertheless not as I will,
but as thou wilt. He went away again the second time,
and prayed, saying, O my Father, if this cup
may not pass away from me, except I drink it,
thy will be done. . .and prayed the third time,
saying the same words.

MATTHEW 26:39, 42, 44

Being God in the flesh, Jesus knew the terrible price He was about to pay for the sin of mankind. He would be accused unjustly, betrayed, denied by one of his strongest followers, beaten, spit upon, mocked, slapped, taunted, nailed to a cross, and crucified. Yet the cup that He dreaded was none of these things; it was that He must become sin as God's sacrificial lamb to pay the price for our sins.

Three times Jesus asked God to let the cup pass from Him, but He prayed for the will of the Father to be done. He addressed God as "Abba," a name of affection and endearment in the closest father-child relationship. He reminded His Father that all things were possible with Him, even to remove this cup. He prayed earnestly and sweat as if it were great drops of blood. His burden of sorrow there in the garden was so heavy that it was worse than death itself; He fell on the ground, and an angel came to strengthen Him. Still, none of the pleadings of God's only begotten and precious Son prevailed in the heart of the Father. And on the cross, Jesus cried out, "My God, my God, why hast Thou forsaken me?" (Matthew 27:46) as the ultimate price was paid, and the Holy God had to turn His face away from His only Son.

God would not answer this prayer of Jesus to take the cup away. It had been planned in heaven with the Father, the Son, and the Holy Spirit that the Son would come to earth as God incarnate and pay the price for our sin. If God had answered, "Yes," we would never have fellowship with Him; we would have no hope; we would have no life. Amazingly, God the Father loved us so much that He said "No" to Jesus, His Beloved Son. He let Him die on a cross to save us and then triumphantly rise again to give us the hope of eternal life with Him!

We should be very grateful that sometimes God answers, "No!"

A RECIPE FOR PRAYER

O give thanks unto the Lord; call upon his name:
make known his deeds among the people.

PSALM 105:1

The "recipe" in the first five verses of Psalm 105 shows us ten ingredients for prayers that please God.

"Give thanks." Before you sleep each night, remember to thank God for the many mercies He has shown you that day. Often we are so busy that we forget His multitudes of blessings.

"Call upon his name." The power of Jesus' name is more than we can imagine. Jesus is the way to reach the Father, and there is no other way given under heaven.

"Make known his deeds among the people." Share the wonderful things God has done for you and for others. It will strengthen their faith and yours, too.

"Sing unto him, sing psalms unto him." Sing the old hymns with their great theology and joyful praise choruses in your heart when you are in the spirit of prayer. It may be in a special prayer time, or it may be as you work. Also, get into the habit of reading the Psalms. They make your heart sing and help you feel close to God as you pray.

"Talk ye of all his wondrous works." Meditate on the things He has done, how fearfully and wonderfully we are made, how everything in nature fits together, how He has provided for us physically and spiritually, and the miracle of God in Christ.

"Glory ye in his holy name." We glory in things that delight us. God delights us!

"Let the heart of them rejoice that seek the Lord." Sometimes our prayers are heavy because our burdens (or the burdens of others) are heavy. Leave your prayer time with rejoicing in good things, and the burdens will lift and joy will return.

"Seek the Lord." Seeking God is as vital to our spiritual life as air and water are to our physical life. Seek Him often. He will always be there waiting.

"Seek his face evermore." To know and observe a person's face is to know the person. You can know God well by reading His Word.

"Remember his marvellous works that he hath done." Remember is one of the most important words in the Bible. We should never forget all God has done for us.

A MAN OF PRAYER

Epaphras, who is one of you, a servant of Christ,
saluteth you, always labouring fervently
for you in prayers, that ye may stand perfect
and complete in all the will of God.

COLOSSIANS 4:12

Epaphras was a teacher and leader of the Colossian church, a faithful minister of Christ, and a fellow servant of Paul. He was even imprisoned with Paul in Rome, but probably the most important part of his ministry was intercessory prayer. When he was traveling with Paul, Epaphras was remembering those back home to God. He prayed constantly; he prayed fervently; he worked hard at being an intercessor. He was permanently passionate about praying for his fellow believers.

We know we should pray for our pastors and deacons just as they should pray for the members of their church. Pastors should for pray their deacons, Sunday school teachers for their class members, music directors for their choir members, nursery coordinators for their workers, senior leaders for the elderly, youth leaders for their youth, Sunday school directors for their teachers, and so on. If we ever begin to complain about our fellow laborers, we should instead ask ourselves how much time we have spent praying for them. What a difference it would make in so many ways! As practicing Christians, it is our responsibility to pray for our fellow workers in Christ.

Epaphras labored fervently in prayer for his fellow Christians. Intercessory prayer is not easy because we share the burdens of those for whom we are praying. It takes our caring, our thoughtfulness, our energy, and our precious time.

Epaphras prayed that his fellow Christians would be mature in their faith and that they would walk confidently in God's will and not be drawn away by Satan. His prayers were simple but powerful. Our prayers for our fellow Christians should be the same.

PLEASE PRAY FOR ME

Brethren, pray for us.

1 THESSALONIANS 5:25

Often friends, relatives, and acquaintances ask us to pray for them. We enthusiastically promise to do so; but sometimes, because of the press of everyday life, we don't remember the person's request until days later or maybe never at all.

Have you ever been embarrassed when someone says, "Thank you for praying for me," but you had forgotten all about it? You meant to pray for them because they were depending on you to call down help from God. You felt you had failed them because you knew the prayers of others had seen you through many difficult situations and in turn others needed your prayers. You determined never to forget again.

So, how can you remember? Write it down! Write it on your grocery list, Sunday school quarterly, a piece of paper in your Bible, the church bulletin, restaurant napkin—anything to keep it in mind until you get home and put it on your prayer list.

Keep a prayer journal because often when you are praying for one person, another comes to mind. Or maybe a friend is already on your prayer list, and you are glad to hear how you can pray specifically for him or her. At the end of the day, ask God to help you remember those you have met and conversed with and pray for them. It will give you joy when someone says to you, "I could tell you were praying for me; it really helped!" or "I knew someone was praying for me!"

Recently a young lady told me that she had thought of me early that Sunday morning and had prayed for me. It just so happened that Satan was working on me that morning, and I was so grateful for her intercession. In my rather long life, rarely has anyone told me they were praying for me; but when they do, I appreciate it enormously.

The apostle Paul often asked Christians to pray for him. He depended on it. Missionaries depend on it. Church leaders and laymen depend on it. Everyone should depend on it! Pray for others just as you pray for yourself, and don't forget!

PRAY FOR MISSIONARIES

Any missionary will tell you the most important thing we can do for them is to pray. We begin to pray and get stymied because we don't know most of them personally or what is happening with them at that moment. We receive prayer letters periodically, but what are their needs on a regular basis? How do we pray? Here are some things for which they need prayer.

- Anointing of the Holy Spirit as they continue to labor.
- Boldness in witnessing, teaching, and preaching.
- Children to be cared for and protected by God.
- Comfort from the Holy Spirit when they are discouraged.
- Commitment to God each day.
- Control by the Holy Spirit each day.
- Dependence on God to supply every physical and spiritual need.
- Devotions with God each day.
- God glorified in everything that happens to them.
- Joy!
- Love for the people to whom they are ministering.

- Opportunities to share the gospel.
- Reliance on God in tense and stressful times.
- Remembrance that they are not forgotten by Christians back home.
- Rest when they become weary from their many tasks.
- Thankfulness, especially in difficult times.
- The unsaved around them having a hunger and thirst for God.
- Victory in Jesus in situations we cannot even imagine.
- Vision of why God sent them there.
- Yieldedness to God each day.

Pray that other believers would not forget them but you pray faithfully for them, too.

TRAVELING ON MY KNEES

And he said unto them, Go ye into all the world,
and preach the gospel to every creature.

MARK 16:15

It takes a special call from God to become missionaries on foreign fields, but they cannot go there on their own. They need other Christians to stay by the stuff (1 Samuel 25:13), which means they need our financial and prayer support so they can be free to preach the gospel. Give generously and pray often for missionaries. God says we shall share in the reward of those on the battlefront (1 Samuel 30:24).

Read and think about these words:

Last night I took a journey, far across the seas;
I did not go by boat or plane; I traveled on
my knees.
I saw the precious people there, with scars and
wounds within,
But God told me I should go; there was oil to pour
for Him.
I said, "Lord, I cannot go and work with such
as these."

He answered quickly, "Yes, you can. . .by traveling on
your knees."
He said, "You pray; I'll meet their need. You call and
I will hear.
Be concerned about the fate of those both far and
near."
And so I tried it, knelt in prayer, gave up some hours
of ease;
I felt the Lord right by my side, while traveling on
my knees.
As I prayed on and saw them helped, the badly
wounded healed,
I saw God's workers' strength renewed, while laboring
on the field.
I said, "Yes, Lord, I have a job. . .My desire Thy will
to please;
I can go and heed Thy call, by traveling on my knees.

SANDRA GODWIN

PRAY FOR OTHER CHRISTIANS

We often do not know how or what we should pray for other believers, but we can learn from Paul. We may know how to pray for specific physical and temporary needs, but we need to pray for the spiritual life of other saints as Paul did and at the same time, we can learn what God desires in our lives.

In the first chapter of Colossians, Paul prayed that the believers in Colosse would:

- Be fruitful in every good work (v. 10).
- Be thankful Christ died for their sins (v. 14).
- Be thankful for the forgiveness of sins (v. 14).
- Be thankful they were changed people (v. 13).
- Be thankful they were Christians (v. 12).
- Let the power of God in their lives make them patient (v. 11).
- Endure the frustrations of life joyfully (v. 11).
- Increase in the knowledge of God (v. 10).
- Learn God's will through the wisdom of spiritual understanding (v. 9).
- Realize the powerful force of God in their lives (v. 11).

- Thank God for their deliverance from Satan's power (v. 13).
- Live a life pleasing to those around them (v. 10).
- Walk worthy of the Lord (v. 10).

In the first chapter of Ephesians, Paul prayed that they would:

- Experience the tremendous power of the resurrection in their lives (v. 19).
- Realize the riches God has given to them in Christ (v. 18).
- Understand the omnipotence of God over all creation (v. 21).

In the first chapter of Philippians, Paul prayed that:

- Their love for God and fellow Christians would grow (v. 9).
- They would live for Christ purely and sincerely (v. 10).

Follow Paul's example and pray for your fellow Christians!

PRAY FOR PREACHERS

And for me, that utterance may be given unto me,
that I may open my mouth boldly,
to make known the mystery of the gospel.

EPHESIANS 6:19

Paul depended on the prayers of other Christians for the energizing power of God to preach the gospel. He wanted to speak boldly for God, as boldly as he had searched out Christians to persecute them before his miraculous conversion. Paul wanted to be articulate in speaking—not so that others would say he was a great orator, but so that souls would come to know Christ and the church would be established among the Gentiles. In fact, Paul did not consider himself a great speaker at all, but he spoke and wrote so well by God's Holy Spirit that the church has constantly referred to his words throughout the centuries.

Paul's ministry was to take the knowledge of the one God and the Messiah, Jesus Christ, from the Jews who had rejected it, to the Gentiles who had no understanding of God's holy sacrifices, the Temple, the Ten Commandments, and other oracles of God. His was a most difficult task, so Paul beseeched the saints to pray for him. He knew he could not do it on his own strength.

Just like Paul, we must realize the necessity of prayer for preachers of the gospel. We must pray regularly for pastors, teachers, missionaries, children's workers, and any believers who are witnessing daily about God's saving grace. We especially need to pray often for our pastors. Interrupted vacations, taking calls in the middle of the night, counseling warring husbands and wives, calming annoyed church members, making hospital and home visits, as well as dealing with countless other situations we know nothing about, are an accepted part of pastors' lives. In the meantime, they must be preparing messages and sermons for the week, which takes hours of their time and much of their energy.

We want our pastor to give us spiritual food and insight into the Bible. No person can do gospel work without the help of God. Their power is in our prayers. We must not fail our pastor as he preaches God's Word, revealing the mysteries of God to us.

Check yourself. How much and how often do you pray for those that preach the gospel, especially your pastor? Pray down the power for them!

PRAY FOR THE SICK

And the prayer of faith shall save the sick,
and the Lord shall raise him up.

JAMES 5:15

Does God really heal through prayer? Those in the scientific world are beginning to realize what believers have always known: that God does heal!

In *Healing Words*, Larry Dossey, M.D., has observed and studied those under his care who had friends praying for them. He tells about a patient of his in Dallas, Texas, who suffered terminal cancer in both lungs. On what Dr. Dossey thought was the last visit he would ever make to this patient's bedside, he found members of the man's church singing and praying. A year later he discovered the man was not only alive and well, but X-rays showed he was totally free from cancer! In further studies, Dr. Dossey found that patients who were prayed for were five times less likely to require antibiotics, much less likely to have congestive heart failure, and were less likely to suffer cardiac arrest.

Recently, an article on a major newscast told of a new perspective on medical care: A doctor's treatment of patients should take into consideration the patient's attitude toward God. They go so far as to say that doctors should ask their patients what they think about God. They have discovered, as Dr. Dossey did, that patients have a much better chance of recovering from an illness if they pray and have prayer support. This is now so strongly believed by the medical world that courses are taught in medical school on this subject.

Though we know God can and does heal, we still must pray for His will to be done. Even if the outcome we hope for is not God's will, we can still have joy and victory and peace.

A pastor, only forty-five years old, was extremely ill. Some church members said they knew God was going to heal him. After many weeks of prayer, God took him home to heaven where he was free from all suffering forever. Was their faith not strong enough? It was strong, but strong faith trusts God to do the very best for His children according to His will. We cannot always perceive God's will until events unfold, and sometimes we don't understand at all; but we trust God anyway—that's faith.

According to God's will, some are healed, but some are not. Either way, all are helped by prayer.

PRAY FOR OUR LEADERS

I exhort therefore, that, first of all,
supplications, prayers, intercessions,
and giving of thanks, be made for all men;
For kings, and for all that are in authority;
that we may lead a quiet and peaceable life
in all godliness and honesty.

1 TIMOTHY 2:1–2

As a pebble thrown in the water produces rings that go outward in unlimited succession, so our life consists of concentric circles. We pray for ourselves, our families, our friends, and our churches, but rarely do our prayers reach to the outer circles of our lives. How long has it been since you prayed for your president, Congress, and other leaders in the government under which you live?

Perhaps we feel that is not in the spiritual realm of our lives to pray for our leaders, but God says it is. Today, some Christian leaders tell us that Christians need to get involved in the politics of the city, county, state, or federal government. Most of us do not have the ability, time, money, or inclination to do so (except to vote) while raising families and serving God in our designated places. No matter how busy we are, though, we can still be involved in government through prayer, and God urges us to do so.

God's love is to all mankind, including presidents, kings, and all others in authority, and He wants us to be concerned about them in prayer. We may not agree with what they do. They may even be evil. But God says to pray for them, to intercede for them, and even to give thanks for them.

In the free world today, we are allowed to criticize our leaders openly, and we do so in abundance. However, it is not becoming for a Christian to constantly criticize and never suggest prayer for leaders that we do not like. God tells us He sets up kings and brings them down. Can we trust that He is in complete control even of the most powerful leaders?

Our leaders really need our prayers, for we have no idea the difficulties they encounter or how many complex decisions or temptations of power and corruption they face each day. If we want better leaders, we must pray for them. Paul says, in so doing, we grant ourselves a quiet and peaceful existence in which we can pursue godliness and honesty.

PRAY FOR AMERICA

If my people, which are called by my name,
shall humble themselves,
and pray, and seek my face,
and turn from their wicked ways;
then will I hear from heaven,
and will forgive their sin,
and will heal their land.

2 CHRONICLES 7:14

BORN AGAIN IN AMERICA! I saw that slogan one day on a shirt and it impressed me so that it comes to mind often. We are doubly blessed by knowing God through being born again and by the privilege of being born in America, the greatest country in the history of the world.

America was founded on Christian principles by God-fearing men, and God has blessed us mightily. But we have strayed, and morally there is little resemblance between Americans today and those of fifty to one hundred years ago. Many citizens of our country are soul sick—sick with sin, selfishness, strife, evil thoughts, ungodliness, wickedness, ingratitude, murder, fornication, adultery, covetousness, deceit, hatred of God, pride, disobedience to parents, and more. Just read Romans 1:18–32.

In many ways America cannot be called a Christian nation, but millions of Christians are serving in various public offices all over the land. Our president is not afraid to say he is a Christian and that the most influential person in his life is Jesus Christ. In the last century, churches in the United States have sent thousands of missionaries all over the world, sharing the gospel of Jesus Christ as well as millions of dollars in medical, material, and financial help. Churches in rural areas, towns, and cities are filled on Sunday mornings with worshipers who give sacrificially of their time, talents, and money to serve the God of the Bible. As we work, Christians must also be sure to spend time praying for this great nation. America can change if the citizens repent and we pray as God tells us to pray.

God says we need to humble ourselves before Him, pray, and seek His face so that our nation will be healed from its soul sickness. Patriarchs of the Old Testament confessed the sins of Israel as though they were their own. They cared that much about God's people. How much do we care? Pray for America!

PRAY FOR ISRAEL

Brethren, my heart's desire and prayer to God
for Israel is, that they might be saved.

ROMANS 10:1

Why would Paul pray for Israel? Because he yearned for their eyes to be opened to the glory of knowing Christ even as God had opened his eyes.

God made Israel His special people, not because they were superior to other nations, but because He was to be glorified through them. He had led them out of slavery in a foreign country to become His people. He mercifully forgave their wicked sins over and over again, but they rebelled against Him over and over again.

The final rebellion against His love and mercy was to reject the Messiah who had been promised for four thousand years. Jesus Christ was the piece of the puzzle that fit perfectly, fulfilling hundreds of prophecies in the Old Testament. Despite His miracles, His teaching, and His love, they said, "No, this is a blasphemer!" Today some of them are still waiting for the Messiah.

Moses pleaded with God to forgive Israel of their transgressions because of His great mercy, and God pardoned them (Numbers 14:19–21). He told Moses that all the earth would be filled with His glory despite their rebellion. It has been and will be. Still, they reject the Messiah.

David's prayer for Israel was, "Wilt thou not revive us again: that thy people may rejoice in thee?" (Psalm 85:6). Still, they rebelled against Him.

Jeremiah's prayer for Israel was, "Do not abhor us, for thy name's sake, do not disgrace the throne of thy glory: remember, break not thy covenant with us" (Jeremiah 14:21). God has never broken His covenant with them. Still, they reject His Son.

It is amazing that Israel has survived for thousands of years and is still the center of the world stage today. God has preserved them because His covenants are everlasting. One day, according to a multitude of prophecies from Genesis to Revelation, they will be His people once more because they will acknowledge Jesus Christ as the true Messiah.

Let us never forget that through the fall of the Israelites, salvation has come to the Gentiles (Romans 11:11), and everything Christians believe is based on the relationship God had with them in the Old Testament. Pray for Israel.

PRAY FOR YOUR ENEMIES

Bless them that curse you,
and pray for them which despitefully use you.

LUKE 6:28

Is there one among us who has not been looked down on, treated with disdain or contempt, intentionally left out, or whose motives have been misjudged at one time or another by our coworkers or family or friends or fellow Christians? God teaches us how to deal with such situations, whether real or imagined. He says to pray for those who do these things. As we shine the light of God's Word on any situation, we begin to see the person or persons involved as God sees them. Only then can we pray for them and show grace toward them as God has shown to us.

In praying, we must examine our hearts and lives to see if we have acted in a manner that causes those who hurt us to react as they do. Many times this is the case; and we need to pray for ourselves first, then pray for those whom we perceive to be our enemies.

Who are our enemies? We cringe at the thought of anyone in our family or church being our enemy, yet this is where we are most likely to suffer hurt because we are living and working together in close proximity.

In the family setting, especially regarding spouses, we are told by "experts" that we need to talk out every problem. This is not always the best advice. Praying about a situation first may prevent us from ever having to talk about it because God will resolve the issue. Try the twenty-four-hour rule. Pray and wait on God for twenty-four hours before mentioning the offense (or supposed offense). You may never even have to bring it up!

Can fellow Christians who tread thoughtlessly on us be our enemies? It seems like they are sometimes, but we must love them, speak well of them, be courteous and friendly, and do good to them. Most importantly, we must pray for them. Let God speak to you through Psalm 37.

Pray for God to forgive those who hurt you and to give you grace to forgive and love them because He loves them. You will find that prayer does change things.

HANNAH'S PRAYER

And she [Hannah] was in bitterness of soul,
and prayed unto the Lord, and wept sore.
And she vowed a vow, and said, O Lord of hosts,
if thou wilt indeed look on the affliction of thine
handmaid, and remember me, and not forget thine
handmaid, but wilt give unto thine handmaid
a man child, then I will give him unto the Lord
all the days of his life.

1 SAMUEL 1:10–11

In Israel, where religion was decaying and neglected, Elkanah was a faithful country priest who went up each year to the temple in Jerusalem to make sacrifices. On one such occasion, his two wives (not permitted by God, but practiced in Israel), Hannah and Peninnah, went with him. Hannah was his favorite wife, but she could not bear children. Peninnah had many children and taunted Hannah about her barrenness.

Hannah suffered much in these trying circumstances and became bitter. But one day in the temple, she turned to God for help in her difficult and hopeless situation. God saw her many tears mingled with her prayers. He saw her heartbreak, disappointment, and guilt as no one else could—heartbreak because she saw no way out, disappointment because her life had not turned out the way she had hoped, and guilt because in those times it was thought that a barren woman had certainly done something to displease God.

Hannah promised God that if He would permit her to bear a child, she would give him back to God all the days of his life. Since the priesthood was handed down from father to son, she knew this promise could and would be accomplished to glorify God.

God saw her tears, knew her heart, and answered her prayers; and in turn, she kept her vow to God. She gave birth to a son and when he was weaned, she returned to the temple and gave him back to God. Her son served God all of his life and became one of the great patriarchs of the Old Testament—Samuel, the great prophet of Israel. His name means "asked of God."

We can find great encouragement that God remembered Hannah and a great example that Hannah remembered God!

A MOTHER'S PRAYER

And Samuel grew, and the Lord was with him. . . .
And all Israel. . .knew that Samuel was established
to be a prophet of the Lord.

1 SAMUEL 3:19–20

We are familiar with Hannah's prayer for a son in 1
Samuel 1, and God answered it in a great and mighty
way. Her son, Samuel, became one of the greatest
prophets in the history of the Israelites, and today we
can still read his words and hear from God.

What do we want for our children? Wealth? Fame?
Prestige? Like Hannah, we should want the very best
God has planned for them.

I do not ask for riches for my children,
Nor even recognition for their skill;
I only ask that Thou wilt give them
A heart completely yielded to Thy will.
I do not ask for wisdom for my children
Beyond discernment of Thy grace;
I only ask that Thou wilt use them
In Thine own appointed place.
I do not ask for favors for my children

To seat them on Thy left hand or Thy right;
But may they join the throng in heaven
That sings before Thy throne so bright.
I do not seek perfection in my children,
For then my own faults I would hide;
I only ask that we might walk together
And serve our Savior side by side.

PHYLLIS DIDRIKSEN

Pray for your children!

PRAYER LEADS
TO ACTION

Lord, what wilt thou have me to do?

ACTS 9:6

Prayer not only has a profound effect upon our relationship with God, it also changes our relationships with other people. While interceding for our neighbor, family member, fellow Christians, or others, God often leads us to do something for that person.

Preachers, missionaries, and others who have committed their lives to God in full-time service have usually heard His call during prayer. Since all Christians should serve God full-time, we need to receive our marching orders while in communion with Him. Our list of people we remember in prayer helps us to keep track of what is happening in their lives and what we can do to help and serve them.

For example, while praying for:

- Susan: Think how you might have an opportunity to speak with her again about taking Christ into her life.
- George: Remember to thank him for the work

he has done in keeping up the sign on the front lawn of the church.

- Katy, who has been missing from church a great deal lately: Plan to call her as soon as possible to encourage her.
- Patti, who is a faithful Christian woman with an amazing sense of humor in the midst of devastating family problems: Send her an e-mail with a cheery word, and remind her that you are praying for her.
- John, who is gravely ill: Remember to call and encourage him.
- Family members: Ask, "What am I doing to show them I care about them?"
- Your Sunday school teacher: Write him or her a note expressing your appreciation for faithful teaching of God's Word each Sunday.
- Your pastor: Remember to regularly tell him how much his sermons mean to you and how you appreciate his concern for his flock.
- Missions: Ask yourself, "How much can I give to further God's work?"
- The church: Ask yourself, "Am I serving God there as much as I can?"

Prayer propels us into a life of service to God and to others.

DON'T FORGET

They forgat God their saviour,
which had done great things in Egypt.

PSALM 106:21

The history of the Israelites in the Old Testament is a picture of human nature. God highlights this in Psalm 106, which includes a litany of the sins of Israel. The Israelites would get into trouble, call on God, expect answers immediately, and then as soon as God's help came, they forgot what He had done. Again and again, they would turn from Him, bring more trouble on themselves, and rush back to Him for help.

They praised Him at times for bringing them out of Egypt and for the wonders He had performed in allowing them to go through the Red Sea. Now and then they believed His words and even acknowledged that their forefathers had sinned in provoking Him. Yet after all that, they turned on God and made a golden calf to worship. We wonder how they could do that, but we do the same things if we are not careful. We praise God for what He has done, but then we put everything ahead of Him. We speak the conversation of the world, seek the pleasures of the day, forget that

He has given us everything we possess, and totally neglect our relationship with Him. Then we expect Him to answer our prayers.

The Israelites forgot God, but they didn't want Him to forget them. They forgot the One who had saved them. They forgot His works and His words and even murmured against Him. No doubt they asked, "Why did God let this happen to us?" They had experienced God's blessings but still whined and complained.

Like the Israelites, we often forget the blessings and care of our heavenly Father. We must not let our relationship with God deteriorate because of our ingratitude and forgetfulness. As we pray, we must continually remember all God has done, all He is doing, and all He will continue to do for us in the future—and thank Him for it!

PRAYING CHRISTIANS ARE HAPPY CHRISTIANS

Be careful for nothing;
but in every thing by prayer and supplication with
thanksgiving let your requests be made known unto God.
And the peace of God, which passeth all understanding,
shall keep your hearts and minds through Christ Jesus.

PHILIPPIANS 4:6–7

Christians should not be serious, long-faced people who never laugh. Actually, the most joyful and fun-loving folks I have ever known are Christians, but let me hasten to say that even many Christians have not found the joy that God has for them because they are not praying Christians. Praying Christians are happy Christians.

Happy Christians have confidence that God knows and cares about every situation in our lives, whether large or small, and can work them out. Therefore, we can approach life with an optimistic outlook, knowing that everything is not necessarily going to turn out just as we hoped, but He will be there to see us through whatever happens.

Happy Christians get along with other people. God teaches us many things in His Word about human relationships. As well as giving us the way to eternal life through Jesus Christ, the Bible is the best psychology book ever written (Philippians 4:8–9).

Happy Christians are grateful for everything in their lives and even see bad situations as learning experiences to trust God. Because we know God sees the end from the beginning, sees around the corner, and knows the whole picture, we have a cheerful outlook about what is happening to us today.

Happy Christians encourage others and in so doing, we encourage ourselves. In praying for others and bringing to their minds the very words of God, we grow in our faith.

Happy Christians depend on God for everything, especially for His guidance in every decision in life.

Happy Christians know they have a Friend in Jesus. What better friend can we have? And we have the blessed, happy hope of knowing that our loving Friend is waiting for us at the end of the way.

Most of all, happy Christians have the peace that passes understanding through prayer.

IN DISTRESS?
CALL ON GOD

Then they cried unto the Lord in their trouble,
and he delivered them out of their distresses.

PSALM 107:6

This verse is repeated four times in Psalm 107. God emphasizes that He wants us to call upon Him in times of great need. In this instance, what had happened to the Israelites to drive them to call on God?

The Israelites were alone and lonely in the wilderness even though they were among hundreds of thousands of people, but they had no city or homes in which they could live. Do you ever feel you don't really belong anywhere and are totally alone? Call on God!

The Israelites were hungry and thirsty and felt weak and helpless in their souls. When you hunger and thirst after righteousness and are feeling very weak in yourself, call on God!

"For He satisfieth the longing soul, and filleth the hungry soul with goodness" (Psalm 107:9).

The Israelites brought trouble on themselves because they rebelled against the words of God and ignored His wisdom. When we stay away from God's

Word, we may wander into bad relationships, quarrel with our coworkers or family, lose our joy, and become depressed about life. In these situations, many seek counsel from a pastor or psychiatrist before they ever call on God and look into His Word for wisdom. When you find that you have ignored or rebelled against God, turn back to Him right away. Call on God!

God sent the Israelites food, and they refused to eat it; then they became ill and approached death. They became afflicted because of their sins, and God said they were fools. Sin brings its own punishment. In today's world, bad habits of eating, smoking, drinking, and other careless behavior brings on ill health. Some approach death long before their time, causing grief to family and friends. Even then, call on God! He will deliver you from your distress. The circumstances may not change, but He will help you through them all.

When the tempests of life toss you about as though you were caught in the terrible waves of a stormy sea, call on God! "He maketh the storm a calm, so that the waves thereof are still. Then are they glad because they be quiet; so he bringeth them unto their desired haven" (Psalm 107: 29–30). God, as your life preserver, will carry you through and bring you to the haven of peace you so desire if you call on Him.

PRAISES FOR
PRAYER TIME

Great is the Lord, and greatly to be praised;
and his greatness is unsearchable.

PSALM 145:3

Praising God in prayer time will bring joy to our hearts, lighten our load of problems, and convince us that God really can take care of everything for us. Are you so burdened with your problems that you don't think to praise Him? The secret of joyful prayer is seeing the face of God through praise. He is worthy of praise!

Praise God for:

- Becoming flesh and dwelling among us: His incomprehensible gift (John 1:14).
- Being our good shepherd to lead us safely home: His guidance (John 10:14).
- Delivering us from hell: His mercy (Psalm 86:13).
- Everlasting life: our future with Him (John 6:40).
- Giving His only begotten son to die for our sins: His everlasting love (John 3:16).

- The water of life so we may never thirst again: satisfaction in Him (John 4:14).
- Giving us the Holy Spirit to dwell in us: strength and comfort (John 14:16).
- Hearing our prayers: refuge (John 9:31).
- His faithfulness: trust (Psalm 89:5).
- His peace: freedom (John 14:27).
- His righteousness: His goodness (Psalm 7:17).
- His Word: knowing Him (Psalm 56:4).
- Knowing He will never turn us away: grace (John 6:37).
- Making us His disciples: experiencing God (John 8:31).
- Not letting us slip: security (Psalm 66:10).
- Praying for us: intercession (John 17).
- The beauty of His holiness: purity (2 Chronicles 20:21).
- The miracle of being born again: being alive to God (John 14).
- The resurrection: proof He is alive (John 20:1).
- The wondrous works of nature: enjoying God's world (Psalm 148:4).

RETURNING TO GOD

Blessed be God,
which hath not turned away my prayer,
nor his mercy from me.

PSALM 66:20

God is kind and merciful and generous to hear our prayers despite our weakness in keeping a consistent, faithful prayer life. Many times our prayers are cold, infrequent, irregular, and only dutiful. We are often hesitant to return to Him after a dry spell of living without prayer, yet God bids us come boldly to Him. Knowing that He has said this is often the only reason we have the courage to approach Him once more.

Even though the first prayer God hears from you is the prayer of repentance when you accept Christ as your Savior, God will hear you and receive you and answer your prayers when you confess your sin of coldness and disinterest and return to Him.

Perhaps you blame your lack of prayer on your busy life, but that is not an acceptable excuse. We cannot wait until all our work is done and then pray, for our work is never finished! The more hectic our lives, the more we need to pray. Prayer produces calmness when we are in a hurry. Ask God to make you calm in the midst of all the busyness of business or all the frustrations of caring for children and family or just being overwhelmed by the details of life.

When you reject God and His love for a short or extended period, you reject answered prayer and have a communication breakdown with Him. Many have broken fellowship with God and don't even realize it because they do not follow the rules and conditions of prayer. Unaware that they are doing something to keep God from responding, they drone on without realizing God is not listening.

Praise God that when you turn from your coldness, apathy, and indifference and back to Him, He will be there and will not turn away your prayers. That is mercy!

THE PRAYER OF JABEZ

And Jabez called on the God of Israel, saying,
Oh that thou wouldest bless me indeed, and
enlarge my coast, and that thine hand might be with me,
and that thou wouldest keep me from evil,
that it may not grieve me!
And God granted him that which he requested.

1 CHRONICLES 4:10

We don't know much about Jabez except that he was an honorable man. He probably had attained some stature among the men of Judah of his day, but he certainly was no prophet or priest or king and was and is relatively unknown. And yet, God answered his prayer and it has been taught, written, and preached about at great length.

Immediately, this is encouragement for the average man who is unheard of except in his circle of acquaintances and friends and yet wants his life to count for God. There are very few believers who stand head and shoulders above the crowd. Most live out their lives in obscurity; yet they are the ones who through the centuries have demonstrated the power of prayer and made possible, through the direction of the Holy Spirit, the furtherance of the gospel. Countless things you accomplish for God may never be known by anyone but you and God—and that's the way God may want it.

Jabez prayed fervently that God would bless him. Intercessory prayer is the highest sort of prayer, but it is not selfish to pray for ourselves, too. God wants us to have all that He has planned for us. We want God to bless our endeavors, to know His power in our lives, and to be free from the evil of sin and trouble, both in our hearts and the world around us. God answered Jabez's prayer to bless him, and He will do that for you if you seek to live a life that is honorable to Him.

Jabez was an honorable man. Did he pray because he was honorable or was he honorable because he prayed? Both should be true. Prayer changes us and makes us honorable and good and righteous and holy. The prayer of Jabez demonstrates James 5:16, "The effectual fervent prayer of a righteous man availeth much."

TWO GARDENS

And they heard the voice of the Lord God
walking in the garden in the cool of the day:
and Adam and his wife hid themselves
from the presence of the Lord God
amongst the trees of the garden.

GENESIS 3:8

Why did Adam and Eve hide from God in the Garden of Eden? Obviously because they had sinned, which produced shame and guilt. God called, "Where are you?" He knew where they were and what they had done, but now they were accountable to Him because they had sinned. Do we hide ourselves from God or let anything and everything keep us from meeting Him in the garden because we know we have willfully disobeyed Him? Adam and Eve tried to cover their sin with fig leaf aprons. We try to cover our sin with excuses that are just as flimsy.

In sinning, Adam and Eve had displayed selfishness, dishonor to God, ingratitude to the One who had not only created them but had also given them a delightful place in which to live, and disobedience to a Master who had shown them nothing but love and kindness. Do we ever let these things come between us and fellowship with God our heavenly Father?

And they came to a place which was named Gethsemane:
and he saith to his disciples,
Sit ye here, while I shall pray.

MARK 14:32

How different from the Garden of Eden was the Garden of Gethsemane located at the foot of the Mount of Olives! Here Jesus suffered the agony of submitting Himself to the will of the Father, the agony of God Himself in the person of Jesus Christ paying for our sin. Here we see honor, obedience, unbroken communion, and boundless love.

We are so like the disciples whom Jesus found sleeping three times, instead of keeping watch in prayer as He had asked them to do in His time of greatest need.

We can learn much from the very different events in these two gardens. Let us not be rebellious, like Adam and Eve, or oblivious, as were the disciples, toward the great God of the universe. But let us meet God openly, honestly and repentant, eager to walk with Him as our God and Friend.

THE SWEET SMELL
OF PRAYER

Let my prayer be set forth before thee as incense.

PSALM 141:2

According to the custom of the priest's office, his lot was to burn incense when he went into the temple of the Lord. And the whole multitude of the people were praying without at the time of incense.

LUKE 1:9–10

We all have our favorite smells. Baking bread, springtime, leaves burning, flowers, sunshine on pine needles, empty churches, or dinner cooking are a delight to us. Likewise, prayer is a sweet-smelling sacrifice to God. It is an offering of our heart to the One who created our soul and then redeemed it from sin. Prayer is symbolized by incense in the Bible. Incense has no odor until it is set on fire, and so our prayers do not have that sweet aroma unless they have the fire of earnestness and enthusiasm.

In the temple service, the hot coals were taken from the altar of burnt offering (a picture of Jesus' sacrifice for our sins) and put on the golden altar, where incense was sprinkled on the hot coals and thus set afire. While the smoke of incense ascended each morning and evening, the priests made intercession for God's people. A symbol of believing and acceptable prayer, it was placed directly in front of the Ark of the Covenant.

Only through the sacrifice of Jesus Christ can our prayers be acceptable to God, for He told us, "No man cometh unto the Father, but by me" (John 14:6). That applies both for eternal salvation and for prayer. Man has tried to think of every way to get to God except through Jesus, but, "He that entereth not by the door. . . but climbeth up some other way, the same is a thief and a robber" (John 10:1).

Prayer is a precious privilege to us and a fragrant smell to God. He delights in our prayers—they give Him pleasure. Often we do not realize how much we are pleasing Him through our prayer life, but He created us for communion and fellowship with Him. He wants to constantly smell the sweet scent of our prayers!

A BOWL OF PRAYERS

Now when He had taken the scroll,
the four living creatures and the twenty-four elders
fell down before the Lamb, each having a harp,
and golden bowls full of incense,
which are the prayers of the saints.

REVELATION 5:8 NKJV

In this heavenly scene of praise to the Lamb who is sitting on the throne, the air is filled with beautiful music of the angels while they offer something of remarkable fragrance to Him in golden bowls. What is it? Our prayers! They are that precious to God! Lest we count our prayers insignificant, let us also consider how important they are to God the Father.

Then another angel, having a golden censer,
came and stood at the altar. He was given much incense,
that he should offer it with the prayers of all the saints
upon the golden altar which was before the throne.
And the smoke of the incense, with the prayers of the
saints, ascended before God from the angel's hand.

REVELATION 8:3–4 NKJV

69

The angels were given incense by Jesus Christ the High Priest to pour on the golden altar (symbolic of the believing and acceptable prayers of the saints), which stood before the throne of God. As the hot coals fired the incense, a wonderful smell came before the throne, but the incense had to be given to them by Jesus Christ. Any other sacrifice—any prayers without Christ—are an unacceptable stench to God; but our prayers in Jesus' name are a welcome aroma.

The saints praying on earth and the angels offering them to God are simultaneous. The angels can only stand by the altar and hand over the bowls. We are the ones who must pray the prayers, and it is the sacrifice of Jesus on the altar that makes our prayers have their sweet fragrance.

This magnificent picture of prayer encourages our hearts to do that which will bless the heart of God. How a sinless God can accept the prayers of sinful man is beyond our imagination. We can only thank and praise Him that it is so!

HOW TO BE STRONG

In the day when I cried thou answeredst me,
and strengthenedst me with strength in my soul.

PSALM 138:3

Have you ever watched Christians go through traumatic experiences and wondered how they could be so strong? They revealed inner strength or strength in their soul, which comes from crying out to God and hearing from Him through His Word.

And God says "in the day," or immediately, we gain strength through communion with Him. Every answered prayer makes us stronger spiritually as we learn to depend on God.

Through prayer, God gives us strength to bear our burdens, not with a downcast face and spirit, but with a smile on our face coming from a cheerful heart.

Through prayer, God gives us strength to resist temptation in the many ways that Satan presents it to Christians, for truly the spirit is willing but the flesh is weak.

Through prayer, God gives us strength to carry out our duties. Each day we face many responsibilities involving countless details. We grow weary and sometimes discouraged, but we can depend on God's promise, "But they that wait upon the Lord shall renew their strength; they shall mount up with wings as eagles; they shall run, and not be weary; and they shall walk, and not faint" (Isaiah 40:31).

Through prayer, God gives us strength to cling to Him and to maintain peace of mind. He gives us the very faith to be saved and to live the Christian life, and it is through fellowship with Him that He carries us through in that faith. If we depend on our weak flesh, we lose the battle, but as 2 Chronicles 20:15 says, "Be not afraid. . .the battle is not yours, but God's."

Children run instinctively into the arms of their mother or father for refuge when they are frightened and need assurance that everything will be all right. God wants us to have that same simple, trusting confidence in Him when the storms of life wash over us— that's how we can be strong.

The Lord is the strength of my life;
of whom shall I be afraid?

PSALM 27:1

ASK FOR WISDOM

If any of you lack wisdom, let him ask of God,
that giveth to all men liberally, and upbraideth not;
and it shall be given him.

JAMES 1:5

We desperately need wisdom. We need it when we are young and making decisions about our futures; we need it when we are grown and working and rearing children; we need it when we move into old age. We make important decisions every day of our lives, no matter what our age, and we need God's true wisdom to guide us through them.

Wisdom is the combination of knowledge and good judgment. When we receive Christ into our lives, we begin to understand the world and the people in it from His perspective. As Christians, we must daily seek God's wisdom and knowledge from His Word. We must want it and pray for it, and God will grant it to us because He has specifically told us to ask for it!

Wisdom can only be built on the foundation of knowledge, but we must be careful that we don't get our knowledge from the wrong sources. Christian books and counseling have their place, but always remember that we need to learn about God directly from His Word first and then go to other sources.

Paul prayed this for all Christians, "That the God of our Lord Jesus Christ, the Father of glory, may give unto you the spirit of wisdom and revelation in the knowledge of him" (Ephesians 1:17).

The fear of the Lord is the beginning of knowledge:
but fools despise wisdom and instruction.

PROVERBS 1:7

For the Lord giveth wisdom:
out of his mouth cometh knowledge and understanding.

PROVERBS 2:6

HINDRANCES TO PRAYER

Behold, the Lord's hand is not shortened,
that it cannot save; neither his ear heavy,
that it cannot hear:
But your iniquities have separated between you
and your God, and your sins have hid his face from you,
that he will not hear.

ISAIAH 59:1–2

Here are some specific spiritual problems that will hinder our prayers:

- A hardened heart (Hebrews 4:7).
- Asking for selfish purposes (James 4:3).
- Gossip and talebearing (Proverbs 18:8).
- Holding on to anger and grudges
  (1 Timothy 2:8).
- Ingratitude (Colossians 4:2).
- Insincerity (Matthew 6:5).
- Lack of domestic tranquillity (1 Peter 3:7).
- Lack of faith or doubting God's Word
  (James 1:5–7).
- Lack of love (1 John 4:20).
- Being lukewarm (Revelation 3:16).

- Not asking according to His will
  (1 John 5:14–15).
- Not being submissive to His will
  (1 Samuel 15:22).
- Not caring about the needs of others
  (Proverbs 21:13).
- Not forgiving others (Matthew 6:14–15).
- Not having a right heart (Psalm 19:14).
- Not praying in Jesus' name (John 15:16).
- Putting other things before God
  (Ezekiel 14:3).
- Self-will (Matthew 26:39).
- Sin (Isaiah 59:1–2).

Constantly seek to avoid these hindrances to keep your prayer life healthy and stay close to God!

BECAUSE WE KEEP HIS COMMANDMENTS

And whatsoever we ask, we receive of him,
because we keep his commandments,
and do those things that are pleasing in his sight.
And this is his commandment,
That we should believe on the name of
his Son Jesus Christ, and love one another,
as he gave us commandment.

1 JOHN 3:22–23

God does not just hand out answers to prayer *carte blanche*, as many believers and unbelievers mistakenly presume. There are conditions to answered prayer, and one is that we habitually keep His commandments and do the things that please Him.

John is not speaking about the Ten Commandments in this passage (although God says they are now written on the tables of our hearts and believers instinctively keep them by walking with God). Here, he is talking about two commandments given by Jesus that move us to a higher plane of living—to believe on God's Son Jesus Christ and to love one another.

First, we must believe in Jesus to gain access to

God at all. There is no other way to have a relationship with God except through His Son.

Second, we must love one another. Real love is not simply the words "I love you." Real love, God's love, is the love described in 1 Corinthians 13. It's a daunting checklist because we fall so short of God's definition of real love. Only by prayer can we press toward that perfect goal of loving as God loves. He says we must love others in order to have our prayers answered. Is there someone in the church you carry an old grudge against? Someone you don't want to speak to? A neighbor with whom you carry on a running hostility? A family member you cannot tolerate? You must rid yourselves of these feelings and let God help you love them as He loves them in order to fellowship with Him.

When you pray, ask God to help you keep His commandments and give you the JOY of loving Jesus first, Others second, and Yourself last!

LOVE ONE ANOTHER

Wherefore I also, after I heard of your faith
in the Lord Jesus, and love unto all the saints,
Cease not to give thanks for you,
making mention of you in my prayers.

EPHESIANS 1:15–16

The Ephesians had much for which to be commended. They had faith in the Lord Jesus Christ and they loved one another. Some may have faith and not love. Others may have love but very little faith. Paul writes in 1 Corinthians 13 that if we have enough faith to move mountains but do not have love, we are nothing. That is a sobering thought!

Paul loved all sorts of Christians: the quarrelsome and worldly Corinthians, the mixed-up Galatians, the rock-solid and loving Ephesians, the generous Philippians, the questioning Colossians, the growing and flourishing Thessalonians, and the eager and teachable Christians in Rome. He loved them, and he loved them enough to pray for them.

As we meet new people, we find many folks who have trusted Christ and find a special bond that we quickly recognize. We are kindred spirits. God has given us the seal of the Holy Spirit, His mark on us, and we quickly identify that mark in others. The sign of a true believer is that he loves other people, and there is a special love among fellow Christians as they share together in experiencing the love of Christ and demonstrating it to others.

God says our love for others is the greatest testimony of our faith. By sharing Christ's love with nonbelievers, we demonstrate His great love for us when He died to save us from our sins; and we create opportunities to tell them how they can come to know that love, too.

The greatest joy of our Christian life is to be loved by God and by other Christians and in turn to share that love with others. Real faith in the Lord Jesus and love go hand in hand. The effectiveness of our prayer life depends on it, for when we love as God loves, we know Him and thus can communicate better with Him. 1 John 4:7 says, "Beloved, let us love one another: for love is of God; and every one that loveth is born of God, and knoweth God."

FORGIVE OTHERS

And when ye stand praying, forgive,
if ye have ought against any.

MARK 11:25

We experienced the freedom and joy of forgiveness when we came to Christ, but are we willing to extend that forgiveness to one who has wronged us? Can we extend the same grace to others that God has granted to us? Have we really meditated on the grace of God? And have we truly experienced it?

If we have truly experienced God's grace in forgiving us for our sins, we should want to extend that grace and forgiveness to those who sin against us. If we do not, we are only hurting ourselves because an unforgiving spirit means broken fellowship with God. Broken fellowship with God means that our prayers have no meaning, and they are not heard or answered. It is an absolute prerequisite for communication with God that we forgive others. "For if ye forgive men their trespasses, your heavenly Father will also forgive you: But if ye forgive not men their trespasses, neither will your Father forgive your trespasses" (Matthew 6:14–15).

Paul instructs us in Colossians to have a heart of

mercy and kindness, humbleness of mind, meekness, long-suffering, forbearing one another and forgiving one another, even as Christ forgave us. In Philippians, he tells us to forget those things that are behind us. We must move on from the shadows of our petty irritations and conflicts and out into the sunshine of love.

Nobody likes to feel used. It is probably one of the quickest ways to get us stirred up to anger. And yet God tells us in Luke 6:28 to "Bless them that curse you, and pray for them which despitefully use you." We must forgive and love our enemies and bless those that curse us to be on praying ground.

If we have anything against anyone, we must forgive them even if they don't care whether they are forgiven or not. We are to forgive as the Lord forgave us, because Christ loved and forgave us while we were yet sinners!

CAN GOD PERFORM
WHAT HE PROMISES?

I will cry unto God most high;
unto God that performeth all things for me.

PSALM 57:2

God always does what He says He will do and always completes what He has begun. The history of the Israelites in the Old Testament is a testimony to that. Oh, the wonderful things He did for them! He gave them a miraculous escape from the Egyptians as they fled across the dry Red Sea, fed them daily with manna in the wilderness, quenched their thirst with water gushing from a rock, put a cloud in the sky to lead them by day and a flaming fire to lead them by night, and gave them victory over the heathen peoples dwelling in the Promised Land. He took complete care of their physical and spiritual needs. Will He do any less for us than He did for His ancient people?

When we come to God in prayer, we must believe and confess to God that we have complete confidence in Him, that we totally depend on Him and know He will carry out what He promises. We must realize that only God can take care of all our needs and believe that He will!

Remember, we are crying out to God Most High, the One who created the entire universe—man, plants, animals, earth, heavens, and all the intricate systems that cause them to work together. Surely our Creator knows our needs and how to care for them!

The psalmist says that he will cry unto God, not just a perfunctory prayer only half-expecting God to answer. No, he will cry from the soul, a fervent prayer, expecting good things from the God of the universe with whom all things are possible.

We must believe that God will perform what He promises. He has proven that He can and He will. Expect great things from God!

CARE-LESS LIVING

Casting all your care upon him; for he careth for you.

1 PETER 5:7

Our cherub choir often sang a little chorus on Sunday that I would find myself humming the rest of the week. It went like this:

> *Why worry, when you can pray?*
> > *Trust Jesus, He'll be your stay.*
> *Don't be a doubting Thomas*
> > *Rest fully on His promise.*
> *Don't worry, worry, worry, worry*
> > *When you can pray.*

Sometimes we adults would challenge each other by changing the words around and ask, "Why pray when you can worry?" because unfortunately that is what believers often do. Worry has no place in a Christian's life, but too often we let it bog us down and take away our joy and attractiveness as Christians.

Our prayer list is a catalogue of worries and concerns that continually surround us, but most of them are situations that we can do nothing about. What a challenge and what a joy to present them to God and let Him work things out! God is specific in His Word. He tells us to cast all our cares upon Him because He loves us. A friend once said, "I can't believe God wants us to bother Him with all these little things in life!" He says He does. What could be more specific than this verse?

No matter how big or small, don't hold on to your worries. Pray and give them up to God, and let Him fill you with peace in knowing that He can and will take care of them!

COMMUNING IN
YOUR HEART

*Stand in awe, and sin not: commune with
your own heart upon your bed, and be still.*

PSALM 4:4

Be still, and know that I am God.

PSALM 46:10

In these two verses, God tells us five important things
that He wants us to do to effectively commune with Him:

- **Stand in awe of Him.** We cannot have communion with God unless we have respect for
  Him and His Word. There is an immense lack
  of awe and reverence for God in the world and
  even among Christians today. How would we
  dress and speak and act in the presence of roy-
  alty or someone we greatly admire? Our reverence and respect for the Most High God
  should be much greater!
- **Do not sin against Him.** Don't keep on sinning. Sin kills our prayer life by choking us off
  from communion with God.

- **Pray, think, and meditate on God and the acts of your own life in the solitary times.** Examine your conscience to see what you have done wrong so that you can repent of it. Meditate on God and His wonderful attributes and strive to honor Him. Before you go to sleep, when you wake in the morning, or during a sleepless night are good times to have conversation and communion with your Creator and your Savior.

- **Be still.** Stop talking so much and listen to what God has to say! When we want a child to hear something important we have to say, we must first get them quiet. They have to stop their crying or complaining. Only then will they hear our words. Many voices of the world are competing for our attention, but we must be sure we take time to listen quietly to what God has to say in His Word.

- **Know that I am God.** As we listen to His voice each day, we begin to understand and appreciate the indescribable greatness of God. It is from that glimmer of understanding that we obtain peace through dependence on Him.

CONFESSING

If we confess our sins, he is faithful
and just to forgive us our sins,
and to cleanse us from all unrighteousness.

1 JOHN 1:9

Confession is absolutely necessary to cleanse us before we can approach a holy God. He cannot hear or answer our prayers through the barrier of sin. The Holy Spirit convicts us of the sin in our lives; therefore, confession should be almost automatic when we begin to pray.

To truly confess our sins means that we don't intend to continue in them. We must realize the damage they do in our lives and the sorrow they bring God as they distance us from Him. We must admit them to God and know that only He can pardon them.

One of the greatest promises of God's Word is that He will forgive us when we confess our sins to Him. In fact, He wants to forgive them. If He did not, He would never have sent His only Son to die in order to forgive them.

Not only does God forgive us when we confess, He also cleanses us. Forgiveness is absolution from sin's punishment, and cleansing is absolution from sin's pollution. That cleansing opens the gate to fellowship with God and all the wonderful spiritual joys He has to offer. It clears our consciences and lightens our cares so that we can have a healthy relationship and satisfying fellowship with Him.

Fellowship with God is a delicate thing, easily broken by sin, just as fellowship with a spouse or friend or relative is easily broken when we hurt them. Thankfully, God is faithful and just to forgive our sin and restore us to Him so that we may continue the fellowship He so desires to have with us—the fellowship He created us for!

When you pray, examine yourself and your life for sins you need to confess and make them right with God.

DAVID'S CRIES FOR HELP

Save me, O God;
for the waters are come in unto my soul.
I sink in deep mire,
where there is no standing:
I am come into deep waters,
where the floods overflow me.

PSALM 69:1–2

In our water-skiing days, the easiest way to get into deep water was to simply jump over the side of the boat. Like a rock, I would sink down quickly when I jumped in. Once, as the water closed over my head, I sank into chilly water too deep to be warmed by the tropical sun, and my feet still did not touch the bottom of the bay. In that instant I wondered if I really were going to come back to the surface again!

Like David in this psalm, troubles pour into our lives and make us wonder if we will ever come back up out of the deep waters and into the sunshine again.

O God, thou knowest my foolishness;
and my sins are not hid from thee.

PSALM 69:5

God knows our sins better than we know them ourselves, but David's confession was necessary before he could receive God's help.

O God, in the multitude of thy mercy hear me.

PSALM 69:13

It is only because of the multitude of his mercy that God heard David or hears anyone. God tells us twenty-six times in Psalm 136 that His mercy endures forever. Grace is God giving us what we don't deserve; mercy is God not giving us what we do deserve.

Deliver me out of the mire, and let me not sink.

PSALM 69:14

When we first began water-skiing, we did not have a ladder to climb out of the water and into the boat. Only a strong masculine arm and hand could pull us up and over the side of the boat. I was not strong enough to pull myself to safety, so I had to depend on the strength of the person in the boat. It is God's powerful arm that helps us. We are too weak to hold on to Him, but His awesome strength holds our hand and keeps us safe. We can only reach up to Him in prayer.

DID YOU ASK?

Ask, and it shall be given you; seek, and ye shall find;
knock, and it shall be opened unto you: For every one that
asketh receiveth; and he that seeketh findeth; and to him
that knocketh it shall be opened.

MATTHEW 7:7–8

How many prayers have not been answered because we have not asked? How many experiences with God are missing in our lives because we do not seek? How many times is the door to God closed because we have not knocked?

In the small church I attended as a child, a stained glass window depicted Jesus standing, knocking, and waiting at the door of a charming little cottage. I can still see the beautiful, vivid colors of the glass, especially His blue robe and rich brown hair. I did not know the true meaning of that picture until I answered His knocking on my heart's door and let Him enter my life. Now, I know that the fulfillment of salvation is to knock on His door in the same manner, ask Him to meet every need, and seek His mercy and grace. He is faithful to open the door so we may enter into fellowship with Him.

Why do we ever hesitate to ask of God? If we have a close, personal relationship with a friend or family member, we don't mind seeking them out, knocking on their door, or asking them for help. Because they love us, we know they will do whatever they can for us. "If ye then, being evil, know how to give good gifts unto your children, how much more shall your Father which is in heaven give good things to them that ask him?" (Matthew 7:11).

God does not mind when we ask of Him; He wants to answer us. He will never turn us away when we seek Him; He wants us to find Him. He is not disturbed when we knock; He wants to open up to us. Do not stop the flow of blessings from God by not asking, seeking, or knocking on His door—we desperately need the Friend who is waiting there to welcome us!

HE HAS ALREADY
ANSWERED

And it shall come to pass,
that before they call, I will answer;
and while they are yet speaking, I will hear.

ISAIAH 65:24

Before we ever called on God for forgiveness of our sin, Christ Jesus had already taken care of it. He paid the price over two thousand years ago. He was just waiting for us to ask. God wants us to know that is true of all our prayers if we are walking with Him. Oh, how this promise increases our faith as we pray!

One day, many years ago, I was laboriously scouring the kitchen stove. It was, no doubt, my least favorite of all household chores, so I was praying while I worked.

That day we had a great need for ten dollars (a considerable sum in those days). I knew we did not have that amount of money and saw no way of getting it. I did not work, we had three children, and our income was about three to four hundred dollars per month.

As I prayed, I timidly reminded God that we had faithfully given Him the tithe that was His; and since He had promised to take care of us, could He please, in some miraculous way, provide the ten dollars.

Before I was finished, the mailman delivered a letter from my husband's mother, who lived fifteen hundred miles away. I opened the letter and a check for ten dollars dropped into my lap! Why was she sending us the money? My husband had left his snow skis in the attic of the family home in Ohio; and since we certainly didn't need them in Florida, she had sold them and had already sent the money before I began to pray!

Our prayers are not usually answered so quickly, but this testimony to the faithfulness of God could be echoed over and over by praying Christians. Our God is a God of promises kept and pre-answered prayers.

Call on Him; He has already put the answer in motion. Help is on the way!

HOW MUCH FAITH
DO WE NEED?

But without faith it is impossible to please him:
for he that cometh to God must believe that he is,
and that he is a rewarder of them that diligently seek him.

HEBREWS 11:6

Hebrews 11 contains a list of people who lived by faith and the things that God accomplished through their lives. They were not supermen or superwomen. They were humans just like we are; they simply trusted God. Faith is discussed and described in many ways, but the only way to understand faith is to experience it.

What does faith have to do with our prayer life? Everything! Faith in God is a firm belief and expectation that He is going to do what He says He will do. It is the greatest hope in the world. The patriarchs of the Old Testament experienced the great power of God through faith, and we can, too. He wants to work out the great and the small things in our lives. For the most part, our lives are a composite of little things, and if we let Him work out the little things, we learn He can work out the big things.

When we see answers to prayer and evidence of

God's work in our lives, our faith in Him grows stronger and stronger. Prayer increases faith, and faith increases prayer.

So, exactly how much faith do we need? Jesus said in Matthew 17:20 that if we have faith as a grain of mustard seed, we can move mountains. Nothing will be impossible for us if we have faith even that small. So then, it is not that our faith is so great, but that our God is so great! The amount of faith we need is the amount to know that God is great enough to do anything through us or for us if only we will let Him. There are mountains in our lives that need to be moved. They can be moved through the prayers of faith, even a little faith.

PEACE THROUGH PRAYER

Be careful for nothing; but in every thing
by prayer and supplication with thanksgiving
let your requests be made known unto God.
And the peace of God, which passeth all understanding,
shall keep your hearts and minds through Christ Jesus.

PHILIPPIANS 4:6–7

God says don't be anxious, apprehensive, stressed, afraid, fearful, panicky, agitated, nervous, troubled, uneasy, disturbed, uncomfortable, worried, or impatient for anything! That covers the spectrum of our fears, doesn't it? We don't like any of these feelings, and we can get rid of them, not just minimize them, by bringing every care to God.

"It's not that easy," you might say. "Surely, He can't expect me to have peace in this particular situation—not this financial problem, not this health problem, not this relationship problem, not this problem with my children—it's too overwhelming!" Yet these problems are exactly what God means because no problem is too great for Him.

Get rid of anxiety when the attitude of another person is unbearable, when there is trouble at home or church or work, when the check doesn't arrive on time, or, yes, even when we lose our keys. He says be anxious for nothing.

Bring everything to God in prayer, earnestly, honestly, expecting God to do what He promises. Are we really honest with God when we ask Him to take care of things? We say we are, but then why do we have that worried look on our face?

Bring everything to God with thanksgiving, not whining, "Why has this happened to me?" Why should it *not* happen to you? Job 5:7 says, "Yet man is born unto trouble, as the sparks fly upward." Every day, everyone has problems, and if we focus on them, our lives will only be filled with more problems. Instead, we must focus on all the things in our lives that we have to be thankful for, and then our problems will not seem so great.

Now here is God's part of the promise: Though we will have problems regularly, He gives us peace that passeth understanding, unbelievable peace in stressful situations. Can we trust God enough that we can thank Him for the loving care He gives us through our trials?

What a relief for those heavy burdens to slip off our shoulders and for distracting thoughts to give way to peace as we give them to God and joy fills our hearts and spills over to others.

PERSISTENT PRAYER

And he said unto them,
Which of you shall have a friend,
and shall go unto him at midnight, and say unto him,
Friend, lend me three loaves;
For a friend of mine in his journey is come to me,
and I have nothing to set before him?
And he from within shall answer and say,
Trouble me not: the door is now shut,
and my children are with me in bed;
I cannot rise and give thee. I say unto you,
Though he will not rise and give him,
[just] because he is his friend,
yet because of his importunity [insistent demands]
he will rise and give him as many as he needeth.

LUKE 11:5–8

The disciples had just asked Jesus to teach them to pray. His response to them included this story demonstrating that they should persist in their petitions to God. He tells about a person knocking at the door of a friend to ask for help for another friend who had been on a journey and needed something to eat. At first the friend did not want to be bothered, but because the

101

person kept on knocking, kept persisting, the friend gave him what he needed.

Don't be afraid to keep asking God for something that we know is in His will. George Müller, spiritual giant of the nineteenth century, built orphanages and fed hundreds of orphans by simply asking God. He never told people about his needs. He once asked God over five hundred times for one specific need, and God granted it in due time.

By persisting in prayer, we create a habit of coming to God for our needs and for help in our troubles, which is exactly what He wants. He wants us to completely depend on Him and to recognize His work as He answers our persistent prayers.

Jesus said even a friend may tell you to go away when you knock at an inconvenient time, but there is no inconvenient time to God. He is always there waiting. Isn't it amazing that we often have no time for God, but the Creator of the universe always has time for us? Don't be afraid to ask, and ask often. Don't be afraid to seek Him, and seek Him often. Don't be afraid to boldly knock, and knock often.

THE PRAYER LIFE OF
GEORGE MÜLLER

During the nineteenth century in England, there were thousands of thrown-away children living on the streets of London. On February 21, 1834, George Müller, twenty-nine years old, was led by God to rescue these children. His vision was to feed, clothe, and care for as many as he could and at the same time give these foundlings the good news of the gospel of Jesus Christ. Thus he began a vast missionary effort based on scriptural principles.

There were other orphanages that were supported by the wealthy, but George Müller believed his orphanage should be a wholly Christian work, based on Scripture and funded only by those who totally supported the cause of Christ. He believed this work of God was to be carried on completely by faith with no debts and only as God supplied the means to do it.

Mr. Müller began with no patrons, no committees, no memberships, and only one shilling in his pocket. He determined to ask no one for financial help but to totally depend upon God through his secret life of prayer. He had learned the power of God's Word to help him live a daily walk that was not only productive but also pleasing to God. These were the foundation stones for a worldwide work that saved hundreds of children and lasted over one hundred years. Mr. Müller not only supported his own missionary work in this way, but contributed to other missionary endeavors— all directly from the hand of God.

During the sixty-three years of Mr. Müller's ministry, more than 7.5 million dollars was poured into the greatest orphan institution in the world through prayer alone. Even as the work continued many years after his death, never was a person asked to contribute money.

Mr. Müller took his life motto from a Scripture he read one evening in his devotions: "I am the Lord thy God. . .open thy mouth wide, and I will fill it" (Psalm 81:10). At that time, he asked God for land, a building, one thousand pounds, and the right persons to care for the children. Immediately, the gifts began pouring in! Mr. Müller kept a written record of the date of the requests and the date of the answers. Sometimes he didn't receive any gifts for weeks, but God's provision always came in time to meet the need. He testified that over fifty thousand specific prayers were answered in his lifetime and that five thousand of those requests were answered on the day he asked.

George Müller's life and ministry are an amazing example of the indescribable power of prayer.

PRAY WITHOUT CEASING

Rejoice evermore. Pray without ceasing.
In every thing give thanks.

1 THESSALONIANS 5:16–18

Paul told the Christians in Thessalonica to rejoice all the time and to keep on praying without letup. Does this mean God wants us to do nothing but pray? Certainly not! Everyday life is busy. We must give necessary attention to family, business, church, and a myriad of other duties. Our families, friends, work, and ministries consume a great deal of our time and energy; but through it all, God want us to pray without ceasing by keeping our hearts and minds in an attitude of constant communication with Him.

To pray without ceasing gives us constant fellowship with God. Never-ceasing prayer, never-ceasing praise, never-ceasing joy, and never-ceasing fellowship are inseparable. By living in constant communication with God, His presence fills our busy lives with peace and joy, no matter what the circumstance.

To pray without ceasing keeps us in constant conversation with God and strengthens our relationship with Him. Just as we must converse regularly with the people in our lives to build strong relationships, we must also talk with God regularly to grow closer to Him.

To pray without ceasing makes prayer as natural as breathing. We are not conscious that we are breathing, but if we stop inhaling and exhaling, life ebbs out of us. Just as our body needs oxygen to survive, our spirit needs fellowship with God through prayer to survive. If we stop praying, our spiritual life ebbs out of us, but if we pray without ceasing, our spiritual lives thrive!

Prayer is an attitude as well as an activity. God knows the activity of prayer is limited, but He wants our attitude of prayer to never cease.

PRAYER PARTNERS

Again I say unto you,
That if two of you shall agree on earth
as touching any thing that they shall ask,
it shall be done for them of my Father
which is in heaven.

MATTHEW 18:19

Many times a prayer request is too personal for sharing in a group. Perhaps it's finances, personal or family problems, or certain illnesses you would rather not discuss in a group setting. In these situations, a prayer partner is a special blessing. A prayer partner will go to God on your behalf with any need. You have no hesitation to ask that person for prayer because you have established a bond for that very reason.

God encourages us to be united in prayer with others for specific requests on any matter—seeking answers and experiencing victory in Jesus. Then when we see what God has done, we can praise Him together.

For many years I taught a "prayer partners" Sunday school class. It was divided up into small groups of three or four couples. A special bond was forged among the groups as they shared needs (usually over the phone) and witnessed God working in their midst. One of the greatest rewards was the closeness that developed from sharing each other's joys and sorrows. When we met on Sunday morning, we praised God for all He had done for us that week. During the time I taught the class, one of the members of the class died a lingering, horrible death; but we all learned much about prayer as we experienced together the comfort and joy of the Lord during a terrible and trying time.

A young pastor I know chose an older lady who is somewhat confined to her home as his special prayer partner—what spiritual insight on his part and what rewards on her part! We all need to find someone with whom we can share our joys and sorrows and prayers and praises. Galatians 6:2 says, "Bear ye one another's burdens, and so fulfil the law of Christ." Find a prayer partner today. You'll be glad you did.

WHAT HAPPENED WHEN
TWO MEN PRAYED

And he said unto him [Cornelius], Thy prayers
and thine alms are come up for a memorial before God.

ACTS 10:4

Peter went up upon the housetop
to pray about the sixth hour.

ACTS 10:9

It was only the Jews who had the knowledge of the one God until after Pentecost; but a cataclysmic change was about to take place. From then on, there would be no difference between Jew and Gentile, but any person who called upon the name of the Lord would be saved. The "mystery" of the church was about to be revealed. Since the Jews had rejected Jesus Christ as their Messiah, it was now the privilege of the Gentiles to take the gospel to the ends of the earth.

Although Paul was chosen to be the apostle to the Gentiles, it was Peter, leader of the church and apostle to the Jews, and Cornelius, a military captain from Italy, who were the instruments of this change. Cornelius, a devout man who feared God, gave generously of his substance and prayed always. He sincerely wanted to know God.

One day while Cornelius was praying, God told him in a vision to send his men to Joppa, find Simon Peter, and bring him back to Cornelius's home. God had some things He wanted Cornelius to hear and appointed Peter to tell him.

In the meantime, God was preparing Peter. One day when he went up to his housetop to pray, God told him in a vision that it was now time to take the gospel to the Gentiles.

Both Peter and Cornelius were obedient to God. They met at Cornelius's house, and Peter spoke to him and all the men gathered there with him about Jesus—His baptism, good works, miracles, death and resurrection, and that only through Him could they truly know God. They believed, the Holy Spirit fell upon them, and they praised God. Even Peter and those who had come with him were astonished at this great work of God!

As we faithfully read His Word and pray, God gives us a vision of the lost world. He brings to mind those we should pray for and witness to, those we should encourage, and those we should support. Great missionary work, whether it is to our neighbor or to the entire lost world, has always been energized by prayer. We must follow the examples of Peter and Cornelius by praying faithfully and obey God's direction in prayer. He will use us in awesome ways when we do!

PRAYER WARRIORS

Prayer warriors are strong, silent combatants who fight spiritual battles on their knees against Satan and for the saints as they labor to serve God. There have been multitudes of these unsung heroes, but the following are a few who have blessed my life.

One that comes to mind immediately is my first Sunday school teacher after I came to know Christ at nineteen. Irene was a powerful teacher and imparted to me her great love for God and His Word. When she came to visit me, she would say, "Let's get on our knees and pray." When we did, we knew that we had been in God's presence!

Joe and Betty Hutton, a remarkable missionary couple, often stayed in our home on their way to the mission field and greatly blessed our whole family. I would hear them at night praying in their room, and we would never part company without sharing a prayer time. They believed God answered prayer, and they lived a life of joy and service to the Lord. He was exceptionally real when you were in their presence.

Another great prayer warrior was Edith Fiddes, a dear friend of fifty years, who was my spiritual mentor in my early Christian life. I remember the way she loved, prayed for, generously supported (out of her meager income), and wrote to missionaries. A sparkling Christian, she claimed the promises of God day by day and lived by them.

Jack Ballard was a man who had worked for the U.S. military intelligence, spoke twelve languages, and had a fantastic sense of humor. He loved missions, worked for a worldwide Christian radio ministry, and spoke for the Gideons in many churches. He prayed for many people twice a day. I was one of those blessed people and felt the power of his prayers as God worked in our Bible class. His wife said she would get so tired praying and ask, "Jack, do we have to pray for all these people again?" But Jack would not stop! What a rare and delightful Christian!

Don is an excellent Bible teacher and exemplary Christian. He travels a great distance to work and prays aloud all the way. In answer to any suspicious glances at stoplights, he just points skyward. You can tell he prays.

These are just a few examples of common, ordinary Christians whose lives of prayer have made a difference. Stop to think about the prayer warriors you know, and thank and praise God for them!

QUENCHING OUR
SPIRITUAL THIRST

As the hart panteth after the water brooks,
so panteth my soul after thee, O God.
My soul thirsteth for God, for the living God.

PSALM 42:1–2

Do we realize how much we need God? We must pursue God as fervently as one of His wild creatures instinctively searches for much-needed water.

Many follow Jesus, but how many pursue Him? There is a great difference in the intensity of these two words. Following may be close or it may be at a distance, but pursuing is aggressive, forceful, and determined, stemming from a desire to be close to God, to thirst for Him. Our thirst and pursuit for God in our lives is as important and necessary as an animal's natural thirst and pursuit for water. Too often, we pursue other things, trying to quench our thirst, but Jesus said, "If any man thirst, let him come unto me, and drink" (John 7:37).

Obviously, Jesus is not talking about physical thirst. When we are hot and tired physically, cold water is what we need to refresh us. However, our soul's only source of refreshment is through Jesus Christ. Only He can make us never thirst again, for He tells us in John 4:14, "But whosoever drinketh of the water that I shall give him shall never thirst; but the water that I shall give him shall be in him a well of water springing up into everlasting life."

James 4:8 tells us that if we draw near to God (seek His water), He will draw near to us (give us the water). How do we draw near? By praying, reading, and meditating on the water of His Word. Drink daily from this fount of living water that He provides. It is easy to recognize where animals have found water each morning because the earth and grass beside the river or watering hole is trampled down as they have quenched their thirst. Our path to God through His Word and through prayer should be just as evident in our lives.

There will be dry times in our spiritual lives when we need to ask God to increase our thirst for Him and to satisfy it, and this is a prayer we can know for sure will be answered. He has promised to quench our thirst and make us never thirst again!

REHEARSING IT TO GOD

And Samuel heard all the words of the people,
and he rehearsed them in the ears of the Lord.

1 SAMUEL 8:21

Samuel was upset with the people of Israel. He was a good priest and a good leader, but his sons were judges and priests who had gone bad, perverting judgment and taking bribes. The people didn't want judges over Israel anymore but a king like all the other godless nations around them. Samuel knew this was displeasing to God.

What did Samuel do? He took the problem to God and "rehearsed" all the facts to Him. He presented all the details and how he felt about them, which is exactly what God wants us to do. Sometimes we are troubled by a situation that we can't do anything about, and we nurse dark thoughts for days before we realize that we need to tell God about it. Yes, of course, He already knows all about it—He is omniscient, but He wants us to "talk it out" with Him anyway. He wants to help us with our problems, but first, He wants us to tell Him about them. He wants us to show Him that we want Him to help us and believe that He can.

It is amazing what rehearsing our problems to God will do: 1) It will solidify the situation in our own mind to help us understand the problem better; 2) it will help us see God's viewpoint of the problem as we read His Word and talk to Him about it; 3) it will assure us that we have taken the problem to Someone who can do something about it; and 4) it will help us realize that it is God's problem, too, for 2 Chronicles 20:15 says, "Be not afraid nor dismayed. . .for the battle is not yours, but God's."

Recently, I talked with a Christian leader who related a particular problem to me. I asked him if he had prayed about it, and he said he hadn't. He had omitted the first and most important step in overcoming any problem we may face.

We gain peace and wisdom through "rehearsing" our problems to God. We don't seem to mind rehearsing them to our friends. Why not take them to God? Our friends may or may not be able to help us, but we know God can!

GREAT PRAYERS
OF THE BIBLE

Read and study:

- Abraham's prayer for a son and God's answer (Genesis 15:1–6).
- Daniel's prayer for the sinful Jews in captivity (Daniel 9:3–19).
- David's prayer for forgiveness (Psalm 51:1–19).
- David's prayer for God's favor (2 Samuel 7:18–29).
- David's prayer for mercy (Psalm 86).
- Ezra's prayer for the sins of the Israelites (Ezra 9:5–15).
- Gideon's prayer for guidance (Judges 6:36–40).
- Habakkuk's prayer for revival (Habakkuk 3:1–16).
- Hannah's prayer for a son who became a great leader of Israel (1 Samuel 1:10– 16).
- Hezekiah's prayer when Israel was invaded by Sennacherib (2 Kings 19:15–19).
- Jeremiah's prayer of faith in prison (Jeremiah 32:16–27).
- Jesus' intercessory prayer for all believers (John 17:1–26).

- Jesus' prayer in Gethsemane (Matthew 26:36–44, Mark 14:35–36).
- Joshua's prayer of remorse over the sins of Israel (Joshua 7:6–9).
- Mary's prayer of praise (Luke 1:46–55).
- Moses' magnificent prayer (Psalm 90).
- Nehemiah's prayer for Israel (Nehemiah 1:8–11).
- Paul's prayer for the Ephesians (Ephesians 1:15–23, 3:14–19).
- Peter's prayer for the church (1 Peter 5:10–11).
- Solomon's prayer for wisdom (1 Kings 3:6–10).
- The disciples' prayer for boldness (Acts 4:24–30).
- The model prayer that Jesus taught the disciples (Matthew 6:9–13).
- The psalmist's fervent prayers to know God (Psalm 119).

THE HOLY SPIRIT INTERPRETS OUR PRAYERS

Likewise the Spirit also helpeth our infirmities:
for we know not what we should pray for as we ought:
but the Spirit itself maketh intercession for us
with groanings which cannot be uttered.

ROMANS 8:26

Jesus promised when He ascended into heaven that His believers would not be left alone in the world. He would send the Holy Spirit to dwell in our hearts forever, and the Holy Spirit would be a great Comforter to us. One of the vital works of the Comforter is intercession between us and God to help us in our prayer life.

God understands us so well that He knows we are often unable to pray as we feel we should. Even the great apostle Paul wrote these words to the Roman church acknowledging that he, too, felt the insufficiency of his prayers. However, we can have great strength in prayer with Jesus interceding for us in heaven and the Holy Spirit interceding in our hearts. Those exalted Intercessors make our prayers understandable and acceptable to God the Father! His provision for our weaknesses is awesome!

Even though we become discouraged with our weak prayers, we can be satisfied and at peace knowing that the Holy Spirit is interpreting our prayers to God. Many times when we are praying for others but don't know their greatest need at that moment, we can depend on the Father, Son, and Holy Spirit to help us.

What are unutterable groanings? They are the communication of the Holy Spirit to the Father. Sometimes our hurts and disappointments are so deep that we cannot discuss them with another person or express them to God. They become the Spirit's unutterable groanings as He helps them to reach through to God. In this way, we can pray without a word being formed in our minds or spoken by our mouths.

The Holy Spirit does not require our prayer to be perfect, either. I remember a man who had just recently been saved from a rough life but when called on was willing to pray aloud in church. His halting, awkward, unlearned, simple prayers were a blessing to all those who heard him because his newborn love for Jesus Christ shone through his words. It is not the eloquence and lovely phrases of our prayers, but the fervency and faith of them that get through to God by the power of the Holy Spirit. Never underestimate the power of the Holy Spirit in your prayer life!

THE LONG AND
THE SHORT OF IT

Beware of the scribes,
which desire to walk in long robes,
and love greetings in the markets,
and the highest seats in the synagogues,
and the chief rooms at feasts;
Which devour widows' houses,
and for a shew make long prayers:
the same shall receive greater damnation.

LUKE 20:46–47

Long, rambling prayers in public tend to make the thoughts of the listeners stray. It is not necessary to name everyone on your prayer list, pray about personal concerns, preach a sermon, or review the preacher's sermon during a prayer in church. It is the effectual, fervent prayer that avails much, not the long and flowery prayer.

Jesus described the Pharisees as hypocritical leaders who enjoyed their important position and the robes of respect that went with it. They wanted everyone to notice how religious they were, but their prayers and their attitudes were disgusting to Jesus. Christians, as well as church leaders, should examine their attitudes and public prayers to see if they are pretentious, hypocritical, or too long.

Charles Spurgeon, one of the greatest preachers of the nineteenth century said, "Long prayers and long sermons tend to quench the fire instead of kindling it. Brethren, in all things has our Lord Jesus given us the best example—also in regard to praying.

"When with His disciples, His prayers were of medium length. In the midst of a large crowd, as at Lazarus's grave and the feeding of the five thousand, His prayer was short. When He was alone with His Father—in the Garden or on the Mount—then He prayed all night.

"So ought ye also to do, dear brethren. Among God's children, make your prayer medium long, as Jesus did when He was about to be crucified. When in a crowd or with the sick or dying or the unfortunate, short. When you are alone with your Father in your secret closet, pray as long as you please."

Our public prayers and public testimony often reveal the kind of secret prayer life and attitude of prayer we maintain. Ask God to help you keep your long and short prayers in the right place!

A BOX AND A BASKET

Therefore take no thought, saying,
What shall we eat? or, What shall we drink? or,
Wherewithal shall we be clothed?
for your heavenly Father knoweth that ye
have need of all these things.

MATTHEW 6:31–32

A young lady kept a small box under her bed. She called it her "God Box." She admitted that she was a worrier and couldn't let go of her large or small problems. When she tried to fix things herself, they somehow went wrong; so she devised a plan to write down anything that was bothering her, fold the paper, slip it into the box, and not think about it anymore. It was a visual reminder that she had put her faith in God to work out life's problems.

The lady dated each piece of paper and occasionally opened the box and pulled out random papers to see what had happened. When a prayer was answered, she kept the paper out of the box, but when a request had not yet been answered, she put it back in the box.

Sometimes a problem was solved right away and sometimes she had to wait. If God said, "No," then she knew He had something else in mind. Instead of letting our problems overwhelm us, we can put them in a "God Box," reminding ourselves to give our worries to God and let Him take care of them for us.

And I will make them and the places round about my hill a blessing; and I will cause the shower to come down in his season; there shall be showers of blessing.

EZEKIEL 34:26

Another Christian woman bought a wire basket and placed a pen and paper beside it. Each day as she thought of something that she was grateful to God for, she wrote it down and put it in the basket. She wrote down answers to prayer or just the simple joys of daily life. Soon the basket was overflowing, and now a large laundry basket takes its place! It has been a blessing to her and to her family.

In God's Word, He often tells us to remember. Remembering what He has done for us encourages us to know that He will continue to answer our prayers.

Whether a box or a basket or a prayer journal or whatever we choose to help us, we must constantly remember to give our worries to God and to concentrate on His blessings. "Count your many blessings, name them one by one. Count your many blessings, see what God hath done" (Oatman and Excell).

A FRIEND OF GOD

And the Lord spake unto Moses face to face,
as a man speaketh unto his friend.

EXODUS 33:11

And the scripture was fulfilled which saith,
Abraham believed God, and it was imputed unto him
for righteousness: and he was called the Friend of God.

JAMES 2:23

Ye are my friends, if ye do whatsoever I command you.
Henceforth I call you not servants;
for the servant knoweth not what his lord doeth:
but I have called you friends; for all things that I have
heard of my Father I have made known unto you.

JOHN 15:14–15

When we have become friends of God, we have moved to the highest plane in our relationship with Him. Who is a friend of God? How do you become His friend? Is every child of God a friend of God? Why was Abraham called a friend of God?

Abraham believed and obeyed God. Believing God makes us His child, but obeying Him makes Him our friend. Friends share feelings, secrets, and experiences. They have affection and love for one another. Friends are our comrades, chums, confidantes, and allies. They would do anything for us, and we would do anything for them. This is the kind of close, personal prayer relationship God wants us to share and enjoy with Him.

Because He recognized Abraham's life of obedience, God asked in Genesis 18:17, "Shall I hide from Abraham that thing which I do?" As our friend, God has kept nothing from us. He shares His secrets, desires, and plans for us and for the future of the world in the Scriptures. He put them there to communicate with us, and He wants us to communicate with Him as a friend.

Jesus says in John 15:15, "Henceforth I call you not servants; for the servant knoweth not what his lord doeth: but I have called you friends; for all things that I have heard of my Father I have made known unto you." Jesus gave His life so that we could be His friends. There is no greater love. As the old hymn says, "What a friend we have in Jesus!"

A PRAYER FOR BOLDNESS

And now, Lord, behold their threatenings:
and grant unto thy servants, that with all boldness
they may speak thy word. And when they had prayed,
the place was shaken where they were assembled together;
and they were all filled with the Holy Ghost,
and they spake the word of God with boldness.

ACTS 4:29, 31

God answered this prayer immediately. He gave the infant church courage by filling them with the Holy Spirit, who empowered them to do God's work and glorify Him.

Why do we need boldness? Because we are afraid of negative reactions to our witness or that we might be considered a fanatic or that we may offend someone? These new believers were not afraid to talk about Jesus. They said, "For we cannot but speak the things which we have seen and heard" (Acts 4:20). They spoke even though their lives were threatened because God gave them boldness to overcome even the fear of death.

How can we have such boldness? Only a fervent desire to speak to others about the wonderful grace of God that we have experienced in our lives will cause us to pray for opportunities to witness for Him and have the boldness to use those opportunities.

If you do not have that desire, pray that God will develop it in you. It is a prayer He will surely answer!

The early believers wanted to rise above self and have fearless courage to testify for Christ. They were excited about what had happened to them, and they wanted to share it! In the face of dangerous threats, they calmly asked God to make them brave and bold. He answered their simple, selfless prayers, and so began the living church.

Ask God to lead you to a special person to share the gospel with and then the wisdom, courage, and boldness to do so. He will never fail to answer that prayer.

A PRAYING CHURCH

The first time we learned about the power of prayer was when my husband and I and our four small children arrived at Central Alliance Church in Miami, Florida. Many churches in those days depended on huge programs, visitation, and gimmicks to grow a church and were successful at it. But at Central, we found that this growing church depended on God and prayer more than anything else.

The first Sunday I heard the choir sing, I was awestruck. I had never felt the Holy Spirit in a service like that before. It was just an ordinary Sunday morning service, but the powerful presence of the Holy Spirit directed us to worship God.

We learned shortly that this was a church whose people depended on God for everything. This was a church that fervently loved missions and gave generously to God for the furtherance of the gospel in foreign lands. This was a church that furthered the gospel at home by living for God and witnessing for Him in the neighborhood and in the workplace. This was a church that had built a lovely edifice for the glory of God and was blessed with unity of spirit and love and laughter and whose Sunday school teachers and deacons loved the Word of God and lived exemplary lives. This was a church where people heard about Jesus and His love for them.

Most importantly, this church was a praying church. Women's missionary meetings were prayer meetings. Wednesday night prayer service was just that—a real prayer meeting with the congregation divided into small groups where individuals poured out their hearts to God for missions, for illnesses, for the church, for the unsaved, and for every other need.

An altar rail across the front of the church welcomed those who had physical or spiritual needs, and others joined them in prayer. If others in the church knew it was an urgent need, there would be ten or twenty or thirty people sitting in the front pews praying for those at the altar long after a service had ended, patiently waiting on God to do His work for His glory.

We have long since moved from that city and church, but often our hearts go back to it and the blessing of learning the power of a praying church. I hope you have learned that lesson, too!

APPROACHING GOD

And I set my face unto the Lord God,
to seek by prayer and supplications, with fasting,
and sackcloth, and ashes: And I prayed unto the Lord
my God, and made my confession.

DANIEL 9:3–4

God instructs and encourages us to come boldly to the throne of grace. Jesus has provided easy access to God, but that easy access does not mean that we may come to Him with sin clinging to us from our daily walk in this world.

Daniel was determined to seek God's face, but he needed cleansing and freedom from sin first. He tells us in this passage how he made his confession of sin.

Daniel came with fasting to show that he was truly sorry for his sins and even those of the Israelites. Fasting is done not to sway God into answering our prayers, but to show that we mean business, to show that we are sincere and have repented of our sins.

Daniel came also with sackcloth and ashes. Sackcloth was outer clothing that was very rough because it was made from the hairy skin of goats. When a person was grieving, he wore it next to his skin instead of the usual soft inner garments. It was uncomfortable, just as sin should be uncomfortable to those who love God and want to approach Him.

Ashes demonstrated worthlessness. When cities had to be destroyed, they were left in ashes to blow away in the wind. Nothing worthwhile was left. We can have beauty from the ashes of our lives when we come to Christ. We are not worthy to approach God, but He can make us worthy by forgiving our sins through His Son.

The psalmist asks, "Who shall ascend into the hill of the Lord? or who shall stand in his holy place? He that hath clean hands, and a pure heart" (Psalm 24:3–4).

How do we get clean hands and a pure heart? "If we confess our sins, he is faithful and just to forgive us our sins, and to cleanse us from all unrighteousness" (1 John 1:9). Then we can approach God boldly.

RESTORE YOUR JOY

Restore unto me the joy of thy salvation;
and uphold me with thy free spirit.
Then will I teach transgressors thy ways;
and sinners shall be converted unto thee.

PSALM 51:12–13

David once had the joy of his salvation, the indescrib-able joy of knowing God and daily walking with Him in a very personal way. Then he committed adultery with Bathsheba and planned her husband's murder. He did not lose his salvation, but he lost the joy of it. Sin had come between him and God. In his plea for forgiveness, David asked God to restore the joy he once had experienced.

It is not just such disastrous sins as adultery and murder that come between us and God. He says in Proverbs 6:17–19 that there are seven things He hates: "A proud look, a lying tongue, and hands that shed innocent blood, an heart that deviseth wicked imagi-nations, feet that be swift in running to mischief, a false witness that speaketh lies, and he that soweth discord among brethren." Any sin, no matter how small we may think it is, can ruin our joy in God because all sin is equally offensive to Him.

Someone once said that our relationship to God in Christ is like a heavy log chain stretching to heaven that is unbreakable. But fellowship with God is like a fragile cobweb that can easily be broken by sin. He made a way to restore that fellowship by the sincere prayer of confession and repentance.

If we do not have joy in our walk with the Lord, there is likely some sin of omission or commission that is building a wall between us. To have joy, we must be free in our spirit. The freedom of knowing we are not holding on to sin but living as God wants us to live.

The old hymn says, "Nothing between my soul and the Savior, So that His blessed face may be seen; Nothing preventing the least of His favor, Keep the way clear! Let nothing between" (C.A. Tindley). That's how you have joy.

David says, "Then will I teach transgressors thy ways; and sinners shall be converted unto thee." Our testimony for God doesn't mean anything to unbelievers until we confess our own sin. The freedom from sin and guilt unleashes joy, and then we can share that joy with others!

BELIEVE IT OR NOT

But let him ask in faith, nothing wavering.
For he that wavereth is like a wave of the sea
driven with the wind and tossed.
For let not that man think that he
shall receive any thing of the Lord.
A double minded man is unstable in all his ways.

JAMES 1:6–8

Let us not be tossed about in a sea of doubt when we pray. Do we believe that God can and will answer prayer even though the answer may not be what we want or expect? Not trusting Him completely, do we try to take matters into our own hands?

Those who have doubts are like the waves of the sea, one moment lifted up by belief, the next moment drowning in distrust; sometimes brought up on the shore of faith and hope, another time pulled down by despair and distress. When we pray this way, we allow the winds of discouragement, depression, frustration, attitudes, and circumstances to control us rather than depending on God to see us through.

In Matthew 14, we read about Peter, who trusted Jesus so completely that he believed He could make him walk on the waters of the stormy lake, and Jesus did! But the moment Peter began to doubt, he began to sink. Peter stopped trusting and let his fear of the wind and the waves overpower his faith in Jesus. Only when Peter cried out again in faith, did Jesus save him. Then Jesus asked him, "Why did you doubt?"

It is an unsettled person who doubts when he prays, and we are only deceiving ourselves when we live that way. Being double-minded means that we think in two different ways—sometimes believing God and sometimes not, but we cannot pick and choose when to believe God! Either we can trust Him or we cannot; and we know from His Word, His many fulfilled promises, His amazing love for us, and His work in our lives that we most certainly can!

He [Abraham] staggered not at the promise of God through unbelief; but was strong in faith, giving glory to God.

ROMANS 4:20

I will therefore that men pray every where, lifting up holy hands, without wrath and doubting.

1 TIMOTHY 2:8

HE IS ABLE TO
ANSWER PRAYER

In order to have confidence that God can answer our prayers, we must realize He is omnipotent (all-powerful), omniscient (knows all), and is omnipresent (present everywhere).

In Job 38, God examines our understanding of Him. He asks rhetorical questions that demonstrate His deity. When we look at God from this perspective, we begin to comprehend that He is certainly able to answer our prayers.

He asks Job (and you and me):

- Can you loose the bands that yoke constellations of stars?
- Can you stop the joy of spring?
- Did you give the instinct to animals to hunt prey?
- Do you understand when and why I send hail and snow?
- Do you know the laws that regulate the seasons?
- Do you know what the invisible origin of rain and dew is?

- Do you know where the water came from to fill the ocean?
- Do you understand the boundaries of light and dark?
- Do you understand the diffusion of light over the earth?
- Have you been through the doors of death?
- Is the lightning at your disposal?
- Where were you when I laid the foundations of the earth?
- Who has made the rain to fall in channels and not in a mass?
- Who can bring the rain in times of drought?
- Who decided how rain was to be formed?
- Who put the boundaries on the seas to stop the waves?

Only One can answer yes to all of these questions, and He is God, the same God who wants to answer our prayers. Meditating on these verses from Job will compel us to worship our amazing God, not because we must, but because we are inspired to by His awesome greatness and power! That's how we know He is able to answer prayer.

IN THE PRESENCE
OF THE KING

Reading God's Word and entering into His presence through prayer on a regular basis will place Him in the right perspective in our lives and put us in the right position before Him.

In thy presence is fulness of joy;
at thy right hand there are pleasures for evermore.

PSALM 16:11

We deny ourselves much joy and pleasure if we do not come into God's presence. God wants us to live the abundant life, and it is generated by prayer, a special daily prayer time, not just hit and miss prayer. Praying to God that way is like just saying "Hi" to people we see regularly but never get to know. Don't miss out on the joy of a close relationship with God. Come into His presence, and get to know the King!

Let us come before his presence with thanksgiving,
and make a joyful noise unto him with psalms.

PSALM 95:2

God loves a thankful heart, and we learn to be thankful by reading His Word and praying. The more we stay away from these two spiritual exercises, reading and praying, the less thankful we will be. God teaches us how to sing and pray in the matchless psalms. They are patterns of praise. Worship the King!

Serve the Lord with gladness:
come before his presence with singing.

PSALM 100:2

Can we sing and be glad even when we are slogging through difficult days? Yes! In coming into God's presence, we experience the soothing oil of the Holy Spirit, which heals our hurts, lifts our spirits, and restores our joy as we sing God's praises.

The upright shall dwell in thy presence.

PSALM 140:13

A brief visit with God only occasionally will not bring joy, gladness, thanksgiving, a singing heart, and the pleasures of being with Him. We must dwell in His presence, making our prayer time a vital part of our everyday lives.

MINDLESS PRAYERS

But when ye pray, use not vain repetitions,
as the heathen do: for they think that they
shall be heard for their much speaking.
Be not ye therefore like unto them:
for your Father knoweth what things ye have need of,
before ye ask him.

MATTHEW 6:7–8

We've heard the voodoo chants, the Islamic prayers, and the repetitious litany of other religions. An old Jewish saying was, "Everyone who multiplies prayer is heard." This says that people will be heard by God simply by repeating their prayers over and over. Jesus tells us bluntly in this verse not to pray that way. It is not necessary to use multiplication of words, for our Father knows what we need before we even ask Him.

It is not praying much, but speaking much that is rebuked here. God is warning us against mindless praying. In the light of other Scriptures, we know that it is not the asking that is reproved here but the manner of asking. Even though our prayers may never be in heathen ritual, we must be careful that our prayers are not mindless.

A friend once said to me, "I don't know if I'm praying for the right things or in the right way." That is not mindless praying, but admitting that God knows the problem much better than we do. When the disciples asked Jesus to teach them to pray, He was quick to do so. The Holy Spirit interprets, Jesus intercedes, and God the Father understands our prayers.

Young children do not make long speeches to their parents when they want something. A need may be expressed by one word from a toddler, and we know exactly what he or she wants. We really know before they ask, but we encourage them to come to us for help. We know our children are helpless, and we are delighted to meet their needs. God says our relationship with Him should be as simple as that.

As children get older, they sometimes ask for things they know they can't have. Sometimes they ask over and over until we have to hush them. We don't like mindless chatter, and neither does God. Just a few meaningful words will do.

We don't need fancy or busy prayers to make God hear us. We must simply approach our heavenly Father with our needs and trust Him to take care of them.

IN THE NAME OF JESUS

And whatsoever ye shall ask in my name, that will I do,
that the Father may be glorified in the Son.
If ye shall ask any thing in my name, I will do it.

JOHN 14:13–14

I once knew a church leader who never prayed in Jesus' name. Each time he began to pray, I hoped that this time he would do so; but it never happened. His prayers seemed lifeless. Had he not read this Scripture? Had he not heard other Christians praying in Jesus' name? Did he not understand the power of Jesus' name?

Jesus said that repentance and remission of sins should be preached in His name (Luke 24:47), and believers would have life through His name (John 20:31). Peter made the lame man walk in the name of Jesus Christ of Nazareth (Acts 3:6). Paul commanded the evil spirit to come out of a fortuneteller in the name of Jesus Christ (Acts 16:18). We are to give thanks in Jesus' name (Ephesians 5:20).

Jesus is God's earthly name. He is Jesus the Messiah or Jesus (the) Christ. Messiah is a Hebrew name for Him. Christ is the Greek word for Messiah. Isaiah said His name would be called Wonderful, Counselor,

Mighty God, Everlasting Father, and Prince of Peace. In the book of John, Jesus is called Son of Man, Bread of Life, Light of the world, Gate for the sheep, and Good Shepherd. In Revelation, He is called the Alpha and the Omega, the Living One, Son of God, Witness, Root of David, Lamb, Shepherd, Christ, Word of God, King of kings, and Lord of lords. We can find over one hundred names for Him in the Old and New Testament that illuminate His character; and experiencing God, we learn that He is all of these names.

Because Jesus humbled Himself, took on the form of a servant, and was obedient even to His death on the cross, God exalted Him and gave Him a name that is above every name (Philippians 2:5–10). Be sure to ask in the powerful name of Jesus if you want God to hear and answer your prayers.

GOD'S ADVICE
TO JOSHUA

This book of the law shall not depart out of thy mouth;
but thou shalt meditate therein day and night,
that thou mayest observe to do according to all that
is written therein: for then thou shalt make thy way
prosperous, and then thou shalt have good success.

JOSHUA 1:8

When Moses died, Joshua became his successor. The book of Joshua opens with God giving Joshua instructions on how to become a great leader of the Israelites. God told Joshua never to turn his back on God's Word but to read and meditate on it day and night so that he would know how to live God's way.

How could Joshua, busy moving the Israelites into the Promised Land, possibly have had time to meditate and pray? He had to provide spiritual leadership, plan the logistics of moving over a million people living in tents, furnish them with food and water, prepare for war, divide the land, command his army, and attend to a myriad of other details. With all of these responsibilities, Joshua had to make time for God. He knew if he didn't spend time with God, he would not do it God's way, which was the only way he could accomplish all he had to do.

In order for Joshua to lead others, he first had to be led by God; to be led by God, he had to know where and how God was leading; and to know God's leading, he had to read and meditate on His Word to hear what He was saying.

Joshua succeeded in his work because he listened to God and let God lead him through His Word. God told him, "Be strong and of a good courage; be not afraid, neither be thou dismayed: for the Lord thy God is with thee whithersoever thou goest" (Joshua 1:9). These words gave Joshua strength and courage for the colossal task God had given him. Too often we plunge into our work before we spend any time consulting God by meditating on His Word—and the victory of the day eludes us.

Could we possibly be any busier than Joshua was? If we are too busy to listen to God, we may very well be too busy.

INTERCESSORY PRAYER

And I prayed unto the Lord my God,
and made my confession, and said. . .We have sinned,
and have committed iniquity, and have done wickedly,
and have rebelled, even by departing from
thy precepts and from thy judgments:
Neither have we hearkened unto thy servants
the prophets, which spake in thy name to our kings,
our princes, and our fathers,
and to all the people of the land.

DANIEL 9:4–6

When Daniel prayed this intercessory prayer, the Israelites had been in captivity in Babylonia for seventy years because of centuries of rebellion and sin against God. Now, he was praying for God to take His people back to the land He had given them—back to Jerusalem, God's Holy City, even though the temple was in ruins.

Daniel is a rare man in the Bible. There is no recorded sin about him. Yet he said, "We have sinned." He had been a faithful, loyal, prayerful, and courageous Jew as he lived in the midst of the Babylonians, a godless people. Yet he confessed his sins though he were as part of the unbelieving, idol-worshipping Israelites who had refused to listen to God and did only what they wanted to do.

The Israelites were his people, and Daniel had compassion on them. He related to them and loved them, and He wanted them to get right with God. He could not make that happen, but he could pray.

Intercessory prayers of Moses, Joshua, Jehoshaphat, and Isaiah on behalf of the Israelites are recorded. Jesus and Paul prayed for believers. They loved God and loved His people. We love God, but often fail to love sinners, both believing and unbelieving. Do we pray for those who are far from God? Or are we judgmental about them? Have we ever asked God to forgive them for their sins? Stephen did when he was being stoned to death. Jesus did when He was hanging on the cross.

Jesus prayed a magnificent intercessory prayer for us that is recorded in John 17. His prayer was unlike those in the Old Testament. He was praying for those that loved God. Daniel was praying for those who did not love God.

There are two kinds of people in the world—believers and unbelievers. We need to be interceding for them both.

THE GREAT INTERCESSOR

Seeing then that we have a great high priest,
that is passed into the heavens,
Jesus the Son of God, let us hold fast our profession.
For we have not an high priest which
cannot be touched with the feeling of our infirmities;
but was in all points tempted like as we are,
yet without sin.

HEBREWS 4:14–15

Until we have gone through a particular situation ourselves, we do not really comprehend the feelings of others. God wants us to know that Jesus, our Intercessor, understands what we are going through as no other person can possibly know. When others do not understand, God understands! Our Creator and Savior knows how we are made and how we think and feel. Why? Because He lived life here on earth, and there is nothing we feel that he has not experienced. Think about it.

He suffered:

- Hatred by religious and political leaders.
- Being called a blasphemer, devil, deceiver, and liar.

- Denial, doubt, and betrayal by His followers.
- Misunderstanding and judgment of His motives.
- Rejection by His own people.
- Laughter, mockery, and taunting.

He was:

- Abused physically and mentally.
- Spit on, beaten with a whip, slapped in the face, struck on the head.
- Condemned to death without a fair trial.
- Disrobed and hung on a crude cross.
- Forsaken by His Father and by His followers.
- Put to death with criminals.
- Buried in another man's tomb.

The unimaginable suffering that Jesus endured to save us proves the love and compassion He has for us. Oh, how grateful we can be that our Savior understands all our hurt and pain and intercedes for us when we cry out in prayer!

LORD, AM I ASKING TOO MUCH?

We can pray about anything and everything—lost items, bad attitudes, safety in travel, enlightenment in God's Word, unsaved friends and loved ones, help for ailing bodies, personal feelings that need fixed, family, jobs, sick people, witnessing, difficult situations, and anything else that life hands out on a daily basis. Do we ask God for too much? Do we ask too often? Is that acceptable to Him? Are we bothering Him? Look at what the Bible says about asking:

- "Whatsoever we ask, we receive of him" (1 John 3:22).
- "And this is the confidence that we have in him, that, if we ask any thing according to his will, he heareth us" (1 John 5:14).
- "And if we know that he hear us, whatsoever we ask, we know that we have the petitions that we desired of him" (1 John 5:15).
- "Ye have not, because ye ask not" (James 4:2).
- "If any of you lack wisdom, let him ask of God" (James 1:5).
- "If ye abide in me, and my words abide in you,

ye shall ask what ye will, and it shall be done unto you" (John 15:7).

- "That whatsoever ye shall ask of the Father in my name, he may give it to you" (John 15:16).
- "Ask, and it shall be given you" (Matthew 7:7).
- "If ye then, being evil, know how to give good gifts unto your children, how much more shall your Father which is in heaven give good things to them that ask him?" (Matthew 7:11).
- "And all things, whatsoever ye shall ask in prayer, believing, ye shall receive" (Matthew 21:22).

Do we have a particular need that we hesitate to ask God about? Don't be afraid to ask. He wants us to, and He has told us to, for He is "able to do exceeding abundantly above all that we ask or think, according to the power that worketh in us" (Ephesians 3:20).

MOSES' CONVERSATION
WITH GOD

And the Lord spake unto Moses face to face,
as a man speaketh unto his friend.

EXODUS 33:11

And the Lord said unto Moses,
I will do this thing also that thou hast spoken:
for thou hast found grace in my sight,
and I know thee by name.
And he [Moses] said,
I beseech thee, shew me thy glory.

EXODUS 33:17–18

As Moses talked with God, he asked God for four things: 1) to find grace in God's sight, 2) to know God, 3) to know the way God would have him go, and 4) to see God's glory.

Moses asked to find grace in God's sight. God replied to Moses, "You have found grace in My sight [you are pleasing Me]. I know you by name." Although Moses had, with the miracles of God, just led six hundred thousand people out of Egypt, he needed to hear that he was pleasing God. Don't we all need to hear that? We can know for sure that we are pleasing God by placing our trust in Jesus Christ. Then, we never again have to wonder about God's grace, but we can experience it!

Moses asked to know God. The amazing truth is that we can know God as well as Moses did, perhaps even better since we are on this side of the cross and have the history of the Israelites and the revelation of the New Testament to enlighten us.

Moses wanted God to show him the way He wanted him to go. Do we honestly and sincerely desire that? If we faithfully read and study His Word, God will show us clearly what His will is for us.

Moses wanted to see God's glory, and He did so by conversing with God. The more we walk and talk with God, the more we, too, will see His glory.

God granted all of these requests to Moses, and he grants them to us, if we ask.

PRAY THE PROMISES

He [Abraham] staggered not at the promise
of God through unbelief; but was strong in faith,
giving glory to God; And being fully persuaded that,
what he had promised, he was able also to perform.

ROMANS 4:20–21

God promised Abraham and Sarah a child. They knew
that according to the laws of nature, it was a physical
impossibility. However, Abraham did not consider that
he was a hundred years old and that Sarah was long
past the child-bearing age. He didn't stagger under the
burden of his unbelief. He fully believed that God
would do what He said He would do.

God has given hundreds of wonderful promises just
for you. Search them out, memorize them, meditate on
them, and claim them in prayer. Don't stagger in unbelief even though your situation seems impossible. Here
are a few to start with:

- "Be of good courage, and he shall strengthen
  your heart, all ye that hope in the Lord"
  (Psalm 31:24).
- "But my God shall supply all your need

according to his riches in glory by Christ Jesus" (Philippians 4:19).

- "But they that wait upon the Lord shall renew their strength; they shall mount up with wings as eagles; they shall run, and not be weary; and they shall walk, and not faint" (Isaiah 40:31).
- "For with God nothing shall be impossible" (Luke 1:37).
- "For whosoever shall call upon the name of the Lord shall be saved" (Romans 10:13).
- "The Lord knoweth how to deliver the godly out of temptations" (2 Peter 2:9).
- "Submit yourselves therefore to God. Resist the devil, and he will flee from you" (James 4:7).
- "The steps of a good man are ordered by the Lord: and he delighteth in his way" (Psalm 37:23).
- "Trust in the Lord with all thine heart; and lean not unto thine own understanding. In all thy ways acknowledge him, and he shall direct thy paths" (Proverbs 3:5–6).

MORE PRAYER PROMISES

- "And it shall come to pass, that before they call, I will answer; and while they are yet speaking, I will hear" (Isaiah 65:24).
- "And whatsoever we ask, we receive of him, because we keep his commandments, and do those things that are pleasing in his sight" (1 John 3:22).
- "He will be very gracious unto thee at the voice of thy cry; when he shall hear it, he will answer thee" (Isaiah 30:19).
- "But thou, when thou prayest, enter into thy closet, and when thou hast shut thy door, pray to thy Father which is in secret; and thy Father which seeth in secret shall reward thee openly" (Matthew 6:6).
- "Call unto me, and I will answer thee, and shew thee great and mighty things, which thou knowest not" (Jeremiah 33:3).
- "Call upon me in the day of trouble: I will deliver thee, and thou shalt glorify me" (Psalm 50:15).
- "For the eyes of the Lord are over the righteous, and his ears are open unto their prayers" (1 Peter 3:12).

- "That if two of you shall agree on earth as touching any thing that they shall ask, it shall be done for them of my Father which is in heaven" (Matthew 18:19).
- "If ye abide in me, and my words abide in you, ye shall ask what ye will, and it shall be done unto you" (John 15:7).
- "If ye shall ask any thing in my name, I will do it" (John 14:14).
- "The Lord is far from the wicked: but he heareth the prayer of the righteous" (Proverbs 15:29).
- "The Lord is nigh unto all them that call upon him, to all that call upon him in truth. He will fulfil the desire of them that fear him: he also will hear their cry, and will save them" (Psalm 145:18–19).
- "The righteous cry, and the Lord heareth, and delivereth them out of all their troubles" (Psalm 34:17).

PRAY WHEN YOU DON'T FEEL LIKE IT

Why art thou cast down, O my soul?
and why art thou disquieted in me? hope thou in God:
for I shall yet praise him for the help of his countenance.

PSALM 42:5

Yet the Lord will command his lovingkindness in the
daytime, and in the night his song shall be with me, and
my prayer unto the God of my life.

PSALM 42:8

Why art thou cast down, O my soul?
and why art thou disquieted within me?
hope thou in God: for I shall yet praise him,
who is the health of my countenance, and my God.

PSALM 42:11

Often when we are going through hard times, we see only the darkness and imagine only dark times ahead. But when we turn to God in prayer, He shows us that isn't true. Prayer turns us from despair as we seek God's face, which is revealed in His Word. We must turn our eyes upon Him if we want the troubles of this world to

159

fade in the light of His love and grace.

When we seek God's face, we find the love that can restore us and the love that can put a smile on our face even in the midst of trial and pain. He is the health of our countenance. The psalmist is saying here, "I shall praise Him for the joy I receive from Him and for the reflection of that joy in my face."

To experience God's lovingkindness is to feel His tenderness, love, warmth, regard, devotion, friendship, respect, endearment, partiality, liking, affection, and appreciation for us every day. As we meditate on these words, it puts a joyful song in our heart in the midst of discouragement. There is hope for the hopeless when we enter into the presence of God. I knew a pastor who often prayed, "Lord, give us a new song in our hearts." God has new joys for us every day if we will only seek Him so He can give them to us.

Anger, frustration, failure, disappointment, sorrow, envy, or jealousy may make us feel like we can't pray, but that's when we need to seek God the most. That's when we can fully experience the hope and the love God has for us!

PRAYERFUL REACTION
TO BAD NEWS

And it came to pass, when I heard these words,
that I sat down and wept, and mourned certain days,
and fasted, and prayed before the God of heaven.

NEHEMIAH 1:4

Let thine ear now be attentive, and thine eyes open,
that thou mayest hear the prayer of thy servant,
which I pray before thee now, day and night,
for the children of Israel thy servants,
and confess the sins of the children of Israel.

NEHEMIAH 1:6

Nehemiah was a captive and slave in a foreign country, a cupbearer of the Persian king. Jewish friends had arrived from Jerusalem, God's Holy City, to tell him the gates of the city were burned, the walls were in terrible disrepair, and the whole city was filled with rubble from the destruction of foreign armies. Nehemiah knew it was due to the sins of Israel, and his first reaction was tears and sadness. Then he fasted and prayed.

Though a slave, Nehemiah had been treated well

161

by the king because he was a good and faithful servant and because the hand of God was upon him. He always had a smile on his face; but one day the king noticed his crestfallen look and said, "Why do you look like that? Do you have troubles or are you sick?" Then Nehemiah did a dangerous thing. A servant was never to address the king, but with an instant prayer to God, he asked the king if he would send him back to Jerusalem to lead in the rebuilding of the city walls.

The king not only sent him back to Judah, but also loaded him down with materials and two letters—one to see him through foreign territory and one for the keeper of the king's forest to give him more supplies to rebuild the walls! Nehemiah remembered the power of God and asked for the impossible for God's glory. God always keeps His promises, and He used faithful, praying Nehemiah to overcome seemingly impossible obstacles in order to keep His pledge that the Israelites would return from captivity at the end of seventy years.

Nehemiah was a man of prayer, and his prayerful reaction to bad news opened the way for a miraculous solution. How do you react to bad news? Like Nehemiah, you should not be overwhelmed with despair, but look to God in prayer.

SINGING AND PRAYING

While I live will I praise the Lord:
I will sing praises unto my God
while I have any being.

PSALM 146:2

My pastor once asked, "What songs do you sing when you pray?" I was speechless for I had never sung during my daily devotions, but he certainly started me thinking about it. He meant singing to God inside your head or in your heart. It is one of the best additions to your prayer life that you will ever experience.

The very best times of prayer are when we are overwhelmed with worship and praise for God and His glorious character and attributes and benefits. Singing alone in the presence of God is an entirely different worship experience from when we sing in public worship services. Sometimes we can only remember a few words or phrases, but God accepts our praise, and we don't even have to have a good voice! Here are some great examples of wonderful praise songs to sing to God:

- Alleluia. . .Alleluia. . .I will praise Him. . .I will praise Him. . .(Traditional).

- Because He lives I can face tomorrow. . . .
  Because He lives all fear is gone. . .(Gaither).
- Crown Him with many crowns. . .(Bridges,
  Thring).
- Fairest Lord Jesus. . .Thee will I cherish, Thee
  will I honor. . .(Willis).
- He is Lord, He is Lord. He is risen from the
  dead and He is Lord. . .(Traditional).
- Jesus. . .Jesus. . .Jesus. . .there's just something
  about that name. . .(Gaither).
- Jesus keep me near the cross, there a precious
  fountain. . .(Crosby).
- Jesus. . .name above all names. . .beautiful
  Savior. . .glorious Lord. . .(Hearn).
- Jesus paid it all, all to him I owe; sin had left a
  crimson stain; He washed it white as snow. . .
  (Hall, Grape).
- O, for a thousand tongues to sing. . .my great
  Redeemer's praise. . .(Wesley).
- Praise God from whom all blessings flow. . .(Ken).
- Praise Him, praise Him, Jesus our blessed
  Redeemer. . .(Crosby).
- Thou art worthy, O Lord. . .(Mills).

These are just a few of my favorites. Add them or
some of your own favorites to your prayer life and worship God in song!

TWO OF ELIJAH'S PRAYERS

Hear me, O Lord, hear me, that this people may know
that thou art the Lord God, and that thou hast turned
their heart back again. Then the fire of the Lord fell,
and consumed the burnt sacrifice, and the wood,
and the stones, and the dust, and licked up the water
that was in the trench. And when all the people saw it,
they fell on their faces: and they said,
The Lord, he is the God; the Lord, he is the God.

1 KINGS 18:37–39

Elijah was the only prophet of God against 450 prophets of Baal that day on Mount Carmel, and a remarkable victory was won! Most of us would like to have that kind of faith—faith that would cause God to perform miracles so that many would believe.

This wasn't Elijah's only victory for God. He raised the son of the widow of Zarephath from the dead. He courageously faced King Ahab and denounced him for his sins and the sins of Israel. God answered his prayer for rain in such an amazing way that he had to ride to Jezreel through a windstorm and drenching rain.

What could possibly disable Elijah's great faith in

God? The criticism and threats of Jezebel, the wicked wife of King Ahab. He fled from her into the wilderness and there he sat under a juniper tree and prayed, "It is enough; now, O Lord, take away my life; for I am not better than my fathers" (1 Kings 19:4).

The last few weeks had taken a lot out of Elijah. He thought surely Israel would turn to God after seeing the miracles of God on Mount Carmel, but they didn't. Although they acknowledged that the Lord was God, they did not repent of their sins. Elijah was dejected and depressed, and his ministry seemed a failure.

Have you ever been tired and discouraged and said to God, "I've had enough, Lord. I can't take any more. All the things I have tried to do for you just don't seem to count." Then we become ashamed of those thoughts, but God understands us. God did not chastise Elijah for his discouragement and his wish to die. No, when Elijah awoke from a nap under the juniper tree, an angel had prepared a meal for him and said, "Arise and eat; because the journey is too great for thee" (1 Kings 19:7). Like Elijah, our journey is much too great to travel alone but not with a loving God to care for us!

BLESS THE LORD,
O MY SOUL

Bless the Lord, O my soul: and all that is within me,
bless his holy name. Bless the Lord, O my soul,
and forget not all his benefits.

PSALM 103:1–2

Almost magically, our hearts are stirred to a spirit of prayer and praise in the first five words of these verses, "Bless the Lord, O my soul," and the stirring continues with "all that is within me, bless his holy name." It is a cry to our soul to praise the matchless holiness of Jehovah God. The phrase "Bless the Lord" is stated twice, which tells us that God wants us to pay attention to these words for they are important.

In praising God, we must "forget not all his benefits." A happy, grateful, prayerful soul is one who never forgets the great blessings we have from God. Just look around you; God has given so many benefits. Feel the very comfort of the room where you sit. Taste the plentiful food and drink. Gaze upon the pictures of your loved ones. See all the treasures that have been given to you. Look out the window and view the wonders of nature God has created for you.

Not only do we have these awesome earthly blessings, Psalm 103 also reminds us of all our spiritual blessings from God. He has forgiven our sins and saved us from hell. He spares us from the punishment we deserve. He has established His throne in heaven and is preparing a place there for us. He strengthens and renews us. Our Creator and Redeemer has shown us such bountiful mercy that we cannot even comprehend it.

God has compassion and grace on those who love Him and promises to love us from everlasting to everlasting! Bless the Lord for all the awesome ways He blesses and loves you, for in blessing God, we bless ourselves. It satisfies Him, and it satisfies our souls.

CHOOSE THE BETTER WAY

But Martha was cumbered about much serving,
and came to him, and said, Lord, dost thou not care
that my sister hath left me to serve alone?
bid her therefore that she help me.
And Jesus answered and said unto her,
Martha, Martha, thou art careful and troubled
about many things:
But one thing is needful:
and Mary hath chosen that good part,
which shall not be taken away from her.

LUKE 10:40–42

Jesus visited the home of Mary, Martha, and Lazarus frequently in the small country town of Bethany. There He found the warmth and comfort and familiar hospitality of a loving family. On this visit and perhaps others, Mary sat at His feet listening to His every word while Martha was "cumbered about with much serving." She was so worried and anxious as she bustled around making everything perfect for the Master that she became irritated with Mary for listening to Jesus instead of helping her. Jesus appreciated Martha's hard work and caring for His needs, but her labor became fussiness, and she forgot the reason for her service. She completely overlooked the joy of Jesus' presence.

Martha let her busyness drive her to frustration and anger. Sometimes those in the service of the Lord do a great job in their work but let their importance and responsibilities overwhelm them so that they become short with others and cold toward God. They are missing a Christ-like spirit, which takes away the effectiveness of their service to God.

Mary had chosen to sit at the feet of Jesus, and He said, "One thing is needful: and Mary chose that good part, which shall not be taken away from her." Do we realize what pleases God? Even more than our work for Him, our fellowship with Him pleases Him the most. There are thousands of everyday tasks that demand our attention, but we must judge their importance and determine our priorities. Nothing should be more important or take priority over our time with God. Only when we put Him first, over everything else, will we have true fellowship with Him and effective service for Him. We must be like Mary, letting our earthly duties wait while we spend precious time with our loving Lord!

DELIGHT FOR YOUR SOUL

*In the multitude of my thoughts within me
thy comforts delight my soul.*

PSALM 94:19

This is the essence of prayer. The writer of this psalm was complaining about the tyranny and godlessness of those in the world around him, but he stops in the midst of his tumultuous thoughts to declare that the presence of God within him gave comfort and delight to his soul.

How can we have comfort and delight in God when our world crashes around us? A multitude of thoughts race through our heads when the blows of life fall on us in quick succession, and we think we surely cannot endure. We question, "How did this happen?" "What if I had done this or that?" "What did I do wrong?" "Why did that person do that to me?" "What will people think?" "What shall I do now?"

As we turn to God and begin to think of His mercy and kindness and love toward us, comfort begins to seep into our heart and takes the edge off of our pain. When we realize that He sees the inconsequential sparrow fall to the ground and we are worth much more to Him, we also realize that He holds us in the palm of His hand and will continue to take care of everything in our life.

How do we turn to God? By opening the Bible and reading His words of love and comfort to us and by talking it all over with Him. The amazing fact is that we love and serve a living God who has many things to say to us. We can claim a personal relationship with Him that delights our soul and enables us to approach Him as we would an understanding and caring friend.

We will have a multitude of anxious thoughts and cares invading our hearts and minds until we turn to God and push them aside with thoughts of Him. Two-way conversation is essential for our peace in times of distress. We can talk to God, but when we let Him talk to us, our thoughts will be centered on Him as a sovereign God, and we will know the many comforts He offers to us to delight our souls!

DELIVERANCE FROM FEAR

I sought the Lord, and he heard me,
and delivered me from all my fears.

PSALM 34:4

David made this statement in his psalm of praise when God had delivered him once again from his enemies. God had not only delivered David from evil but also the fear of evil. He will do the same for us.

We fear many things in our lives. As children, we fear the dark; as teenagers, we fear we will not be accepted; as young adults, we fear we won't meet the right lifetime mate; as young parents, we fear for the safety and health of our babies; as parents of teenagers, we fear they will make the wrong decisions and ruin their lives; as middle-aged adults, we fear for the problems of our married children and for the health of our parents; and as senior citizens, we fear for our health and that we will become dependent on our children.

Fear is a powerful thing, and, if we give into it, can overwhelm and paralyze us. The psychological damage from fear retards our spiritual growth and can be debilitating in itself, causing mental and physical illness. But God gives us an antidote for fear: "The angel of the

Lord encampeth round about them that fear him, and delivereth them" (Psalm 34:7).

God says if we fear Him instead of people and circumstances, angels will build a hedge around us and deliver us. It is a great comfort to realize that if we trust God daily, He will take care of us and deliver us from the awful burden of fear. He can even deliver us from the fear of displeasing Him because He gives us exact instructions in His Word about how to please Him.

David said in this psalm that he sought the Lord. Those who communicate with God and express their fears to Him will be heard and delivered. The angels of the Lord encamp about those who have respect, reverence, and awe of Him and who seek His help.

Have you sought the Lord about the latest fear in your life? He will deliver you!

EXPECT ANSWERS

Peter therefore was kept in prison:
but prayer was made without ceasing
of the church unto God for him.

ACTS 12:5

God was blessing the early church in a mighty way. Immediately after Pentecost, when the Holy Spirit came as Jesus said He would, there was healing, cleansing, signs and wonders, and powerful preaching. Thousands came to Christ. Even Cornelius, the Roman centurion, and his household were saved.

However, Herod had had about enough of this; and to please the unbelieving Jews, he killed James, the brother of John, and threw Peter in jail. The believers prayed effectual, fervent, unceasing prayer for Peter. After all, he was one of the great leaders of that spirit-filled infant church, and they needed him desperately! While they were praying, God intervened. He sent a bright, shining angel to the prison who slapped Peter on his side and told him to get up! Peter's chains fell from his wrists, and the angel told him to put on his shoes and cloak and follow him out of the prison. Peter couldn't believe what was happening to him. He thought he was dreaming!

When the angel left Peter, he went to the house of John Mark's mother, Mary, where a prayer meeting was in progress. They heard a knock at the gate and sent a young lady, Rhoda, to see who it was. Approaching the gate, she recognized Peter's voice; but in her excitement, she forgot to unlatch the gate. She left him standing outside while she ran back to the group to tell them their prayers had been answered, and Peter was at the door!

No one believed Rhoda! While Peter stood waiting, they were inside arguing with Rhoda that what she was telling them couldn't be true. She insisted it was Peter and finally convinced them to unlock the gate. When they saw Peter, they were amazed and let him in, and he told them how God had freed him from prison and that they must go tell others.

Those early believers had seen God do great things, and yet Rhoda had a difficult time convincing them God had answered their prayers. How much faith do we have that God really will answer our prayers as He says He will? Expect answers from God!

GETTING TO KNOW GOD

Grace and peace be multiplied unto you
through the knowledge of God, and of Jesus our Lord,
According as his divine power hath given unto us
all things that pertain unto life and godliness,
through the knowledge of him that
hath called us to glory and virtue:
Whereby are given unto us exceeding great
and precious promises: that by these ye might
be partakers of the divine nature.

2 PETER 1:2–4

"Getting to know you, getting to know all about you" is a line of a song that was popular years ago. It's also exactly what God wants us to do with Him. Salvation is free through God's mercy, but getting to know Him requires the focus and discipline of prayer and reading and paying attention to His Word.

Peter prayed for those who had trusted in Jesus Christ that they would have not only grace and peace, but an abundance of grace and peace. We experience more and more of these two precious commodities— more undeserved favor, more calmness and serenity as the storms of life wash over us—as we grow in the knowledge of God. If we have already experienced a portion of God's love, joy, grace, and peace through the forgiveness of sins, we should be encouraged to ask Him for more of these blessings so that they will be multiplied many times over and we can know Him better.

The power of God has given us everything we will ever need in life for godly living. We just need to search out His exceeding great and precious promises so that by these we can be partakers of the divine nature. We are not born with a spark of divinity in our hearts. Growing to be like God comes from becoming His child by trusting Jesus Christ as our Savior and then living a life of trust in what He says. We cannot live spiritually until we are born spiritually, and then we grow spiritually on the food of His precious Word and promises.

God has given us a countless number of precious promises that lead us from faith to virtue to knowledge to self-control to perseverance to godliness to brotherly kindness.

Thus we partake of His divine nature and truly get to know Him—all about Him!

JEREMIAH'S PRAISE
FROM PRISON

*Ah Lord God! behold, thou hast made the heaven
and the earth by thy great power and stretched out arm,
and there is nothing too hard for thee.*

JEREMIAH 32:17

Jeremiah had been put in prison for prophesying the fall
of Jerusalem; and even at that moment, the Babylonian
army, ready with their battering rams, surrounded the
walls of the city. Yet God told Jeremiah to buy his
cousin's parcel of land and bury the deed in an earthen
jar for the day when Jerusalem would be restored again.
God said Jerusalem would be conquered, but the
Israelites would possess it again. Jeremiah perceived
those messages as conflicting. He faithfully delivered
them; but he was confused, and so he prayed.

Today it seems to be okay to question God, to be
angry with Him, to be disappointed in Him, and to give
Him human qualities instead of realizing that He is
the sovereign God of the universe. Although Jeremiah
had to be at a low place in his life—imprisoned, in distress, and not understanding what God had told him,
he burst forth with praise of the Almighty God because

he truly understood who God is.

Jeremiah said to God:

- No one will ever forget that You brought us out of Egypt.
- Nothing is too hard for You to do.
- You have created the universe with Your mighty power.
- You have given us this land even though we disobeyed You.
- You have judged Your erring children impartially.
- You have shown Your love to thousands.
- You see every act that men do.

Instead of crying and whining to God, Jeremiah climbed to the higher ground of praise and never mentioned his distress to God. God assured him that nothing was too hard for Him, that although Jerusalem would be conquered by other nations and His chosen people scattered all over the face of the earth, one day He would gather them from all countries to dwell safely in the land. In our generation, God has done just that!

Keep on praying! Keep on praising! If God could do this miraculous thing for a wayward people, you know He can do impossible things for you through prayer.

PRAISING GOD
IN NATURE

Bless the Lord, O my soul.
O Lord my God,
thou art very great;
thou art clothed with honour and majesty.

PSALM 104:1

We are created to praise God and our hearts lift in involuntary praise as we read the poetry of Psalm 104, which glorifies God for His magnificent creation. God gives us so much to think about in describing Himself in this psalm. We are not left to wonder what He is like or what He has done but are given specific descriptions of the glories of His creation so that we may know how to praise our Creator.

I know a woman who said she did not need to go to church but worshipped by meditating among the trees in the forest. She had no thought of Jesus Christ, though, for we do not find Him in the forest but in the Bible, where we learn to worship the Creator of the forest. He directs us specifically to the perfection of His creation and how each part complements another. Just a few of the glories of God's creation that we should worship and praise Him for are:

- Sun, moon, and stars—He stretched out the starry heavens like a curtain (v. 2).
- Oceans—He hollowed out the surface of the earth and made the seas (v. 3).
- Clouds are His chariots, and He walks on the wings of the wind (v. 3).
- Angels are His ministers of flaming fire (v. 4).
- Fresh water springs out of the mountains, goes down into the valleys, and gives drink to all animals and to the birds, which sing in the trees (vs. 10–12).
- Grass feeds the cattle; herbs feed man; food is brought out of the earth (v. 14).
- Fruits, vegetables, and grains grow to produce wine and oil and bread (v. 15).
- Trees produce sap and make homes for birds as they sing among the branches (vs. 16–17).
- The sun measures the days, and the moon measures the months (v. 19).
- The night is for wild beasts to feed, and day is for man to work (vs. 20, 23).
- Earthquakes make the earth tremble; the mountains belch lava (v. 32).

PRAYER FROM THE PITS

And at midnight Paul and Silas prayed,
and sang praises unto God: and the prisoners heard them.
And suddenly there was a great earthquake,
so that the foundations of the prison were shaken:
and immediately all the doors were opened,
and every one's bands were loosed.

ACTS 16:25–26

Not only had Paul and Silas been beaten and thrown into prison, but their feet were put in stocks. They were no doubt sore and hurting and had to sit in an uncomfortable position with no room to move—not to mention the fact that it was midnight, and they were surely exhausted. In spite of all this suffering, Paul and Silas began singing praises to God.

Our attitude might not have been like that of Paul and Silas. They were praying and singing from the pit of a prison cell! Would we have prayed and praised God from that dirty dungeon? Can we pray and sing and praise God in difficult times when we have been misused or abused, feel uncomfortable and exhausted, or feel trapped in our circumstances?

Paul and Silas sang and prayed and expected God

to hear and answer, and He did! He sent a miraculous earthquake that shook the foundations of the prisons, threw open the doors, and even loosed their bonds. But instead of rushing out of the prison when the doors flew open, Paul stopped and took time to tell the jailer about Jesus. The jailer and his whole family were saved, and he was so grateful to Paul for giving him the gospel, that he took Paul and Silas to his house, cared for their wounds, and fed them.

How did God answer the prayers of Paul and Silas in these awful circumstances? He moved the earth, freed them from their bonds, opened the prison doors, kept the jailer from committing suicide, changed men's hearts, saved the jailer and his whole family, gave them all great joy, and sent them personal care and comfort!

Prayer and praise can bring miraculous earthquakes in our lives, too, even from the pits.

SENIORS CAN PRAY

The righteous shall flourish like the palm tree:
he shall grow like a cedar in Lebanon.
Those that be planted in the house of the Lord
shall flourish in the courts of our God.
They shall still bring forth fruit in old age;
they shall be fat and flourishing;
To shew that the Lord is upright: he is my rock,
and there is no unrighteousness in him.

PSALM 92:12–15

How old is old? Some folks feel old at fifty or sixty. Others don't feel old even at seventy, and there are many folks living healthy and happy lives in their eighties! An abundance of jokes, humorous stories, and philosophical ideas are put forth about growing older. We like to laugh about it, but it is a serious business, especially with the many illnesses that can attack us as we age. Our bodies give out, our faces get lined, our memories grow dim, and we are not sorry to leave this planet and go to our heavenly Father. Thankfully, as Christians we can look forward to eternal life in heaven and a new, perfect body that will never age!

Here on Earth, no person ages more beautifully

than those who have honored and served God all their lives. We often see a huge old oak and exclaim, "Look at that tree! Isn't it beautiful?" Age does not diminish the tree's beauty, nor does age diminish the beauty of a Christian. Older Christians are like trees planted by the rivers of Living Water. Their skin may be withered, but their spirit is not; and they are still growing spiritually as their roots absorb nourishment from the Water of Life. They have demonstrated to the world that the Lord is their Rock and it is good to serve Him.

Many seniors search for things to do to keep their minds occupied and their hands busy, and that's good; but there is something older people can do that is more important than anything they have previously accomplished for the Lord. They can pray! There is a tremendous need in this world for prayer warriors. Seniors have more time to read God's Word, meditate on it, and intercede for friends, family, and fellow Christians than anyone else in their little corner of the world. It is such a simple ministry, yet so powerful and so necessary.

Prayer requires discipline, work, and faithfulness. The last work of saints may be their greatest work and produce the best fruit of their entire lives!

THANK GOD FOR
CHRISTIAN FRIENDS

I thank my God upon every remembrance of you.

PHILIPPIANS 1:3

I have you in my heart; inasmuch as both in my bonds,
and in the defence and confirmation of the gospel,
ye are all partakers of my grace.

PHILIPPIANS 1:7

Recently I received a letter from a Christian friend that I had not heard from in a year and a half and probably have not seen in over twenty-five years. It gave me untold joy and brought a smile to my face for the rest of the day. It started me thinking about the Christian friends my husband and I made over our lifetime and with whom we were "partakers of grace" together. How grateful I am for them! I haven't seen many of them for years and usually only exchange Christmas cards, but that doesn't keep me from thanking God for them.

I remember their dedication to God's work—teaching Sunday school; serving as deacons; singing in the choir; loving, supporting, and praying for missionaries; witnessing to the lost; faithfully attending church;

letting the Holy Spirit control their lives; and most of all sharing their love of Christ. How their lives defended and confirmed the gospel!

I remember and thank God for the many blessings of my Christian friends—the times together of joy and laughter and prayer and praise; their encouragement through cards, letters, and conversations; their ministry to us in time of despair; their patient acceptance of our quirks and faults; and their prayers and support for us in our personal lives as well as our endeavors for Christ. Today I can still feel their loving spirits and enduring friendships.

A few have gone to be with the Lord, but most still live in scattered places around the country, and God continues to bring new friends into my life. I thank God upon every remembrance of old and new Christian friends and look forward to sharing our eternal joy together with Christ.

Take time to think of all the Christian friends God has blessed you with, and pray for them and praise God for them. What an important part of prayer—thankfulness for our friends in Christ!

THE JOY OF PRAYER

Hitherto have ye asked nothing in my name: ask,
and ye shall receive, that your joy may be full.

JOHN 16:24

Do we really want to live a joyful, happy Christian life?
That's what God has planned for us. Some take life so
seriously that they think there is no joy and fun in the
Christian life. It has been said that laughter is joy bub-
bling up out of the heart. And what makes the heart
joyful? Being in close contact and communion with
God, which equals a good, consistent prayer life, a life
of freedom and liberty in Christ.

Prayer is work—sometimes heavy work. We know
our prayers must agree with God's Word. If we get rid
of the hindrances to prayer, weed out bad feelings
toward others, confess our sins, care about the unsaved,
and spend time in His Word, much can be accomplished through our prayer life. It requires discipline of
time and energy, but it also means we are able to share
our victories and defeats with a God who really cares.
Peace, love, and joy are some of our rewards from
prayer. God doesn't want us to miss the joys of an
abundant prayer life any more than the joys of heaven.

A joyful prayer life is praying for results, seeing God work in our lives and the lives of others, and getting excited about it! It is great joy to share an answered prayer with a friend or a prayer group. We call it praise time. Look over your prayer journal. Have any prayers been answered? I have counted at least fifty answers to prayer in the past three months in mine. These were things I asked for specifically and do not even include unwritten requests or simple prayers I whispered to Him throughout the day.

"Ask and ye shall receive," proves God and brings joy. He wants our joy to be full. That means awash with joy, brimming with joy, laden with joy, and experiencing complete and unlimited joy!

Many Christians go through life cheerless and gloomy as though being a Christian is a burden to them. They have not discovered the joy of daily fellowship with God. Don't be one of them! Learn to say with Isaiah, "I will greatly rejoice in the Lord, my soul shall be joyful in my God" (Isaiah 61:10).

A PROGRESSION OF PRAYER

How long wilt thou forget me, O Lord? for ever?
how long wilt thou hide thy face from me?

PSALM 13:1

When we pour our heart out to God as David did in
this psalm, He won't condemn us for it. In his mind,
David knew God had not forgotten him; but in his
emotions, he felt God wasn't there for him. David was
afraid, and fear causes us to doubt and mistrust the very
God who is taking care of us. Such thoughts may come
into our minds and hearts, but we must not entertain
them for very long.

How long shall I take counsel in my soul,
having sorrow in my heart daily?
how long shall mine enemy be exalted over me?

PSALM 13:2

David had sorrow in his heart daily because he took his
eyes off God and trusted the counsel of his own heart.
During trials and trouble, we think they are going to
last forever; but when they are over and we look back,
they seem to have lasted only a moment. We need the
joy of trusting God through our trials, and they won't

seem as long. David did not have the indwelling Holy Spirit, as believers have had since Pentecost, who gives us strength that David never had. But still, we get mired down in self-pity.

Consider and hear me, O Lord my God:
lighten mine eyes, lest I sleep the sleep of death;
Lest mine enemy say, I have prevailed against him;
and those that trouble me rejoice when I am moved.

PSALM 13:3–4

Notice the change that is taking place in the heart of the prayer. He has moved from despair, hopelessness, and defeat to petitioning God for help. He is asking God to give him the light of hope that through the eyes of faith he may look beyond his troubles.

But I have trusted in thy mercy; my heart shall rejoice
in thy salvation. I will sing unto the Lord,
because he hath dealt bountifully with me.

PSALM 13: 5–6

And now his prayer turns into praise. David has come up out of the pit of self-pity and defeat to the joy of victory because he remembers that when he has done so in the past, God has poured out His blessings on him. Have we experienced this progression of prayer and remember to trust God and gain back our joy in Him?

THE PROUD AND
THE HUMBLE

Two men went up into the temple to pray;
the one a Pharisee, and the other a publican.
The Pharisee stood and prayed thus with himself, God,
I thank thee, that I am not as other men are, extortioners,
unjust, adulterers, or even as this publican.
I fast twice in the week, I give tithes of all that I possess.
And the publican, standing afar off, would not lift up so
much as his eyes unto heaven, but smote upon his breast,
saying, God be merciful to me a sinner.
I tell you, this man went down to his house
justified rather than the other:
for every one that exalteth himself shall be abased;
and he that humbleth himself shall be exalted.

LUKE 18:10–14

Everyone wants their prayers to be heard by God, but
many choose to do it in their way and not God's way.
There are prayers that reach God and prayers that do
not reach God. Jesus told this parable to teach us the
difference.

God does not hear our prayers when we try to convince Him how good we have been, how much better

we are than other people, what we have done for Him in the past, or what we will do for Him in the future. The Pharisee believed that because he had lived a righteous life (in his eyes), God owed him something. He went to the temple to pray, but when he arrived there he did not really pray. Prayer is a spiritual communion with God that includes confession of sin, praise, and thankfulness. The Pharisee made no confession of sin but only listed the sins he did not commit. He ignored the fact that arrogance and self-righteousness are terrible sins! The only thing the Pharisee was thankful for was that he was better than other men. Instead of praising God, he praised himself. He did not need God. Following his own rules, he was complete in himself.

In sharp contrast, how did the publican pray? He confessed his sin with a sense of unworthiness and shame, and he pleaded for God's mercy on him. This man went home totally changed because he saw his need for God and called on Him for mercy. God justified him rather than the Pharisee, who with pride and self-righteousness lifted himself up before God. We must be like the publican and humbly bow before God, begging for mercy, and let Him lift us up!

THE SECRET LIFE OF
A CHRISTIAN

But thou, when thou prayest, enter into thy closet,
and when thou hast shut thy door,
pray to thy Father which is in secret; and
thy Father which seeth in secret shall reward thee openly.

MATTHEW 6:6

James Thurber wrote "The Secret Life of Walter Mitty" in which a henpecked husband escaped a dull and frustrating life by pretending that he was a fearless pilot, a brilliant doctor, and other brave and daring characters.

God teaches us in His Word that we, too, should have a secret life, but not one such as Walter Mitty enjoyed. Walter Mitty tried to escape the frustrations and dullness of life by fantasizing. Our secret life is to seek the reality of God in personal, private prayer so that we may fellowship with Him and pursue the joys and excitement of our life in Christ.

God sees and hears us in our secret place. The Pharisees loved to pray in public so everyone could see how pious they were. It is good and necessary to pray in public, especially in church; but the believer who is truly seeking the heart of God will back that up with private prayer.

For in the time of trouble he shall hide me in his
pavilion: in the secret of his tabernacle shall he hide me;
he shall set me up upon a rock.

PSALM 27:5

It is in that secret place where God hides us until we gain our strength, experience joy, and praise Him. It is there we obtain mercy and find help, where we learn His ways, and where we are cleansed and delivered from sin. It is there we learn to wait for Him to act on our behalf. Our body is the tabernacle of God, and the secret place is where He lives in our heart.

He that dwelleth in the secret place of the most High
shall abide under the shadow of the Almighty.

PSALM 91:1

Those who live a life of communion with God live a life of serenity. The storms will wash over them, but their feet are on the Rock. When we are sinking into deep water, we search for a solid foothold. We find that foothold of peace in the secret place of private worship in our hearts.

Walter Mitty's secret life was an escape from reality. Our secret life, hidden in Christ, gives us strength to live out the harsh realities of life with thanksgiving and praise to God.

VISUALIZE

I saw also the Lord sitting upon a throne,
high and lifted up, and his train filled the temple.

ISAIAH 6:1

Then said I, Woe is me! for I am undone;
because I am a man of unclean lips,
and I dwell in the midst of a people of unclean lips:
for mine eyes have seen the King, the Lord of hosts.

ISAIAH 6:5

Isaiah saw God in His glory and holiness and was never the same again. We need to see God that way with our spiritual eyes, and we need to see Him that way in our prayer life. We need to see the King and comprehend how unworthy we are to approach Him yet able to approach Him because God made it possible through Jesus Christ.

We do not have the kind of visions that God sent to Jacob, Isaiah, Daniel, and other patriarchs of the Bible, as well as Peter, John, and Paul in the New Testament; but there are times we need to "see the Lord sitting upon a throne, high and lifted up." We can do that by reading about Him in the Bible.

Sometimes we listen to another Christian pray in church, but we don't really hear the prayer. Picture the congregation kneeling before God at His throne as He listens to the petitions of the person praying aloud. It will help you focus on the prayer and realize you are in the presence of Almighty God.

At particularly low times when you seem to need God's comfort, visualize His loving arms around you; and like the hymn says, find yourself "leaning on the everlasting arms."

In Psalm 148, God tells the angels, sun, moon, stars, waters, mammoth creatures of the deep ocean, fire, hail, snow, fogs, stormy wind, mountains, hills, fruit-bearing trees, coniferous trees, wild beasts, cattle, creeping things, flying fowl, kings, princes, judges, young men, young women, old men, and children to praise Him. Visualize each of these creations praising God.

God paints vivid word pictures in the Bible to help us know Him better. Read His Word and visualize Him in His glory as you pray and praise Him!

WATCH AND PRAY

Watch and pray, that ye enter not into temptation:
the spirit indeed is willing, but the flesh is weak.

MATTHEW 26:41

In the past couple of decades, the world has witnessed the downfall and disgrace of more than a few spiritual leaders. We can't help but wonder about the prayer life of each individual. One naturally thinks that people in such positions spend a great deal of time in prayer, but it becomes evident that some do not when they fall into sin and out of dedicated servanthood to God.

When Jesus spoke these words, He was exhorting His disciples to be faithful in prayer. He was aware of the betrayal of Judas, knew Peter would deny Him, and that the other disciples would desert Him in His darkest hour. He knew that in the flesh, it is easy to fall into sin, although we think we never will, for 1 Corinthians 10:12 says, "Wherefore let him that thinketh he standeth take heed lest he fall."

"Could you not watch with me one hour?" Jesus asked His disciples. He didn't ask them for all night, just one hour! When He desperately needed their prayers, they were sleeping; yet in His great love and compassion, He gave them an excuse. They had nothing to say for themselves, and so He told them He knew they meant to do the right thing despite their weak humanity. He knows how we are made because He created us. He knows that our bodies don't keep pace with our souls.

After the arrival of the Holy Spirit at Pentecost, the apostles totally changed and immediately prayed, preached, and served God in great power. Then they knew how to truly watch and pray.

As we watch and pray and read and study God's Word, we are filled more and more with the Holy Spirit. The willing spirit begins to overcome the weak flesh, and we do not so easily enter into temptation.

Watch your temptations. Pray for help.

WHAT A DIFFERENCE
A PRAYER MAKES

My voice shalt thou hear in the morning,
O Lord; in the morning
will I direct my prayer unto thee,
and will look up.

PSALM 5:3

Making time for fellowship with God in the morning is vital to our spiritual life!

We are fresh and clear of mind, revived and refreshed from sleep. It makes a great difference in our busy schedule when we look up to God the first thing in the morning.

At times we feel chained to the earth in our work or caring for our family, and the day is eight or more hours of drudgery. Prayer brings freedom from the mundane when we are aware that God is there with us. We can experience deep satisfaction even if we pray briefly in the morning; and then once we have started the conversation with Him, continue it off and on throughout the day. It makes life richer, sweeter, and more peaceful. It doesn't mean that bad things will never happen, but God will help us to remain cool and serene in the midst of daily problems as we keep in touch with Him.

Keep in mind the words of this poem:

I got up early one morning and rushed right
*   into the day;*
I had so much to accomplish that I didn't have time
*   to pray.*
Problems just tumbled about me, and heavier came
*   each task.*
"Why doesn't God help me?" I wondered. He
*   answered, "You didn't ask."*
I wanted to see joy and beauty, but the day toiled on,
*   gray and bleak;*
I wondered why God didn't show me. He said,
*   "But you didn't seek."*
I tried to come into God's presence; I used all
*   my keys at the lock.*
God gently and lovingly chided, "My child, you
*   didn't knock."*
I woke up early this morning and paused before
*   entering the day;*
I had so much to accomplish that I had to take time
*   to pray.*

UNKNOWN

JESUS' PRAYER FOR US

I pray for them: I pray not for the world,
but for them which thou hast given me;
for they are thine.

JOHN 17:9

The model prayer in Matthew 6 is usually referred to as "The Lord's Prayer," when actually "The Lord's Prayer" is Jesus' prayer for us in John 17. This is what Jesus prayed for God to do for all believers in all ages:

- Keep them through the power of Your holy name (v. 11).
- May they have the unity of spirit that You and I have (v. 11).
- May they be filled with My joy because of hearing My words (v. 13).
- Even though they are in the world, keep them from evil (v. 15).
- Make them pure and holy through Your words of truth (v. 17).
- I pray not only for present believers, but for future believers who will trust in Me because of the testimonies of those living today (v. 20).

- May all believers have unity of heart and mind so the world around them will know You sent Me to die for their sins (v. 21).
- Help them to live as mature believers and walk with Me so that unbelievers will know You love all men (v. 23).
- May they see My glory, both now and in the future (v. 24).
- May unbelievers know that You love them as You have loved Me (v. 23).
- May we all have a glorious reunion in heaven so they can behold the glory that You have given Me (v. 24).

"Wherefore he is able also to save them to the uttermost that come unto God by him, seeing he ever liveth to make intercession for them" (Hebrews 7:25). How encouraging to know that Jesus is sitting at the right hand of God today praying for us. His prayer reveals how much He loves us and why He gave His life for us.

THE MODEL PRAYER

Lord, teach us to pray, as John also taught his disciples.

LUKE 11:1

Just as you who are reading this book want to know more about prayer, the disciples wanted to know how to pray and asked Jesus to teach them. In answer, Jesus gave them the "Model Prayer." It is commonly called "The Lord's Prayer," but the Lord's prayer is Jesus' prayer for us in John 17. The "Model Prayer," usually read from Matthew 6:9–13, is Jesus' specific example of prayer and our best instruction on how to pray God's way.

There are seven petitions in the "Model Prayer." The first three have to do with God. We are to pray that 1) His name will be honored, 2) His kingdom will come soon, and 3) His will be done here as it is in heaven where He is glorified.

In the last four requests, Jesus taught us to pray for ourselves that God will 1) supply our daily needs, 2) forgive us for our sins, 3) keep us from drifting into those things that would draw us away from Him, and 4) keep us from Satan and all his evil.

The "Model Prayer" demonstrates to us how a

prayer does not have to be long to be heard by God. It is short, compact, and powerful. Every word, every phrase is loaded with what God wants us to know about Him and how He wants us to pray.

In many churches this prayer is repeated at every morning worship service as a rite or ritual and often without meaning. Everyone wants their daily needs to be met, their sins to be forgiven, and to be kept from evil. But do those who recite the prayer in a mechanical way really want to live in God's kingdom? Do they really want God's will to be done in their life? Do they really hallow God's name?

God hears the stumbling prayers of the new Christian, the half-finished prayers of those weary and hurting—every prayer that is uttered. But as in all other aspects of our Christian life, He gives a perfect pattern to follow in prayer. In these last several chapters, let's look deeper into this "Model Prayer" that Jesus gave us so we may learn to follow His example and be sure we are praying His way.

OUR FATHER

Our Father which art in heaven.

MATTHEW 6:9

God allows us and teaches us to call Him Father. Christianity is the only religion in the world that claims a personal relationship with God. Christianity is not a set of rules, a wealth of rites and rituals, man's philosophy about God, or a vague belief in an almighty being or indistinct power to call on when life overwhelms us. It is becoming a child of God through the sacrifice of Christ.

Only those who have trusted Jesus Christ as their personal Savior can call God Father. There is no other way, and the Bible reiterates it from Genesis to Revelation. Jesus insisted that, "No man cometh unto the Father, but by me" (John 14:6).

Many unbelievers mistakenly think that every person born on this planet is a child of God, but this is not true. Would God need to tell us how to become His child if at birth we already were His child?

Neither does being religious make one God's child. Jesus said to the controversial Pharisees, "Ye neither know me, nor my Father: if ye had known me, ye should have known my Father also" (John 8:19). He was speaking to the ultrareligious leaders of God's chosen people, the Israelites. Today, they would pastor large churches, practice religious counseling, visit the sick, preach attractive sermons, write books about spiritual things, and call God Father. How dare He confront them with these accusations? But despite all the evidence in the Scriptures, they did not believe that Jesus was the Messiah, and they rejected the only Way to become a child of God, the only Way to call God Father.

God delights in His "little ones" calling Him Father. We are a joy and pleasure to Him if our daily walk is that of a child who wants to make his father proud of him. We need to have an Abba relationship with God—not one of fear (Romans 8:15), but that of a child walking closely with his daddy and the familiarity of climbing onto his lap. Our relationship is not that of a servant, but a son (Galatians 4:7), a son who has the security of knowing he is loved and cared for by his heavenly Father!

HALLOWED BE THY NAME

Our Father which art in heaven,
Hallowed be thy name.

MATTHEW 6:9

The best and foremost way to hallow God's name is to trust Him to save us, then walk with Him, glorify Him, and praise and reverence Him. The moment we trust Him with our eternal soul, He becomes our heavenly Father. Never before New Testament times had believers been allowed or instructed to call God "Father."

The patriarchs of the Old Testament had reverent, respectful, obedient relationships with God, but they never experienced the warmth and closeness that is revealed to those who approach him through His Son, Jesus Christ. But even with that loving relationship, God is still the Almighty Jehovah, the great, everlasting Creator who demands our utmost respect and reverence for Him and for His name.

God's name is to be regarded as sacred, though, sadly, the third commandment is continually broken today. It is common for many people, even children, to exclaim "My God!" as a byword in their conversation. Even some Christians are guilty of that.

I once worked closely with a good Christian woman who used God's name in vain often. Unsure of what I should do, I prayed about how to approach the problem. Finally, I was asked to teach a Bible study where she was present. One evening we discussed this prevalent problem, without any personal references, in the light of the Scriptures. I never heard her use God's name in that manner again.

There are more than one hundred wonderful names of God given in the Bible. Each of those descriptive names gives us another reason to honor, hallow, and praise Him.

THY KINGDOM COME

Thy kingdom come.

MATTHEW 6:10

God's kingdom has existed ever since the earliest times when Enoch walked with God, when God promised Abraham that from him would come a great people, when God constantly dealt with His unruly and disobedient Israelites, and when Jesus, the promised Messiah, came and declared, "The kingdom of heaven is at hand."

Then, at the death, burial, and resurrection of Jesus, the dynamic power of the kingdom became evident. The Holy Spirit came at Pentecost and the power of the risen Christ propelled the kingdom into a magnificent new age when the gospel went forth to all the earth, and the church was made up of believers in whom the Holy Spirit lived.

But there is more to come! The return of Jesus Christ, the rapture of the church, the terrible tribulation, the millennium, the great white throne judgment, and finally heaven. As Christians look forward to the "everlasting kingdom of our Lord and Saviour Jesus Christ" (2 Peter 1:11), we look with longing and joyful anticipation to that wonderful day when God will make everything right. Jesus said we are to pray for that kingdom to come.

We need to remember that Matthew is written particularly to the Jews, and Jesus is speaking to them about prayer. They were to pray for God's kingdom to come in the sense of looking forward to the millennial kingdom when the Jews as a nation would finally accept Jesus as their Messiah, ushering in the golden age of the fulfillment of all the hundreds of prophecies in the Old and New Testament concerning them.

The next event for Christians in God's kingdom will be the rapture of the church, "For the Lord himself shall descend from heaven with a shout, with the voice of the archangel, and with the trump of God: and the dead in Christ shall rise first: Then we which are alive and remain shall be caught up together with them in the clouds, to meet the Lord in the air: and so shall we ever be with the Lord" (1 Thessalonians 4:16–17).

Thy kingdom come. This prayer will one day be answered for Jews and Gentiles!

THY WILL BE DONE

Thy will be done in earth,
as it is in heaven.

MATTHEW 6:10

When we first come to God through Christ, we see God in a new way. As we begin to walk daily with Him and love Him, our desire to see His will done grows. What is God's will for man? It is this:

- All wickedness would come to an end (Psalm 7:9).
- The desires and motives of all men would pass the testing of God (Psalm 7:9).
- The just would be honored and become strong (Psalm 7:9).
- The righteousness of God would be the standard of man's heart (Psalm 7:9).
- We would comprehend His holiness and see His face clearly (Psalm 67:1).
- All nations would understand how graciously God deals with man (Psalm 67:2).
- Everyone would know and understand God (Psalm 67:2).

- All nations and people would praise God (Psalm 67:3).
- God would be the righteous judge of all people (Psalm 67:4).
- God would govern all the nations of earth (Psalm 67:4).
- God would bless the whole earth (Psalm 67:6).
- The earth would yield abundant harvests (Psalm 67:6).
- Everyone on earth would have reverence for Him (Psalm 67:7).
- His holy name would be blessed by everyone forever (Psalm 72:19).
- The whole earth would be filled with His glory (Psalm 72:19).

Sounds like heaven on earth, doesn't it? Do we love God enough that we would really like to see all these things happen? Jesus prayed, "Not My will, but Thine be done." We must also sincerely pray this prayer with faith that God's will is good and perfect because He knows best.

GIVE US THIS DAY OUR DAILY BREAD

Give us this day our daily bread.

MATTHEW 6:11

God wants us to come to Him for our physical as well as our spiritual needs. Christians must learn that God cares about each and every part of our lives, no matter how big or small. I have heard some say, "I didn't think God wanted to be bothered about those little things." He does; and here, Jesus teaches us to ask even for our daily food.

Our daily physical needs are of utmost importance to our spiritual being. We cannot live without food on a regular basis. God made us that way and then He told us to ask Him for it each day. We then thank Him as we receive it because we recognize that one more time He has blessed us with His outstretched hand.

Psalm 68:19 says, "Blessed be the Lord, who daily loadeth us with benefits, even the God of our salvation." When we look around us, we realize that we are loaded down with all the good things God has given us. This prayer reminds us that daily He takes care of us, daily He gives us food, daily He pours out physical and spiritual blessings upon us.

It is awesome to think about the Israelites wandering in the wilderness because of their sin, yet God feeding them daily with manna—what a miracle! The only strings attached were that they had to obey God's instructions: They should gather only enough food for one day or the manna would rot, except on the sixth day when they could gather enough to cover the Sabbath. God did this so that they would have to keep trusting Him every day. He wanted them to only gather enough for one day at a time, so that the next day they would again have to depend on Him to provide.

God wants us to depend on Him like the Israelites had to do. Jesus is teaching us in this prayer to live our lives depending on God one day at a time. When we pray, we should ask God to provide for that day's needs only, so that the next day we must come to Him again in prayer.

FORGIVE US OUR DEBTS

And forgive us our debts, as we forgive our debtors.

MATTHEW 6:12

Is there anyone, no matter what they believe, who does not want their sins to be forgiven and the heavy burden of guilt removed? God created a conscience in us that speaks from our innermost being. Even agnostics or atheists have some sense of sin and realize that they are responsible for it.

Man has devised many ways to try to remove sin and placate God. Adam and Eve thought they could cover their sin with fig leaves. Cain brought the fruits of his labor to God. Man has always tried to please God by good works such as helping the poor, going to church, baptism, rites and rituals, and even prayer and Bible reading.

Through all this clutter of what man thinks he must do to receive forgiveness, God has said over and over, the only way is to ask for forgiveness through Jesus Christ. God determined the price, and it has already been paid. We cannot get through to God until we have acknowledged sin, repented, and asked forgiveness His way. When we do, He promises that "he is faithful and just to forgive us our sins, and to cleanse us from all unrighteousness" (1 John 1:9).

Is there anyone in your life that you have never forgiven for even the smallest offense? Have you ever heard anyone say, "I can never forgive them for what they have done"? Be careful, for God says it is a dangerous thing not to forgive others. One of the greatest hindrances to prayer is an unforgiving spirit. We must examine our lives and look at how much we have sinned against God, yet how readily He forgives us. Then, because He forgives us, we must also forgive those who sin against us. Ephesians 4:32 says, "And be ye kind one to another, tenderhearted, forgiving one another, even as God for Christ's sake hath forgiven you."

Only when we forgive others can we begin to truly understand the amazing grace of God to forgive us!

LEAD US NOT INTO
TEMPTATION

And lead us not into temptation, but deliver us from evil.

MATTHEW 6:13

After our sin is forgiven, the natural and next thought is that we would not and should not return to that sin again. Yet we know we will be tempted to sin the rest of our lives, albeit less and less, as we walk with God each day.

Do not be confused by this prayer, for God never leads us into temptation. The sense of this petition is that God would lead us away from temptation so that we would not deliberately walk or accidentally stray down that road. When we are tempted, it is not from God, because God never sins and doesn't want us to sin (James 1:13–14). Our own wants and wishes pull us into sin—the desire for things we see, our physical appetites, and our always-present pride. The sources of temptation are Satan, the world, and the flesh.

Temptation does not necessarily always lead to sin, but all too often we take the path of least resistance, and the result ranges from a bad mistake to an overwhelming failure. So we need to "watch and pray, that ye enter not into temptation" (Matthew 26:41).

We find great comfort and encouragement in these words: "There hath no temptation taken you but such as is common to man: but God is faithful, who will not suffer you to be tempted above that ye are able; but will with the temptation also make a way to escape, that ye may be able to bear it" (1 Corinthians 10:13). God does not leave us to deal with temptation on our own. He knows our weaknesses and our limits, and if we let Him help us, no temptation will ever be too great for us to resist.

We also need deliverance from the evil one—his lies, his deceit, and his tricks. Satan is constantly, without letup, planning and plotting to entrap us. He is more powerful than we are but not more powerful than God, for we know that "greater is he that is in you, than he that is in the world" (1 John 4:4).

The power of Satan in our lives can be broken by God. We can keep from entering into temptation and sin. With prayer and watchfulness, He is faithful to lead us away from temptation and deliver us from evil.

THINE IS THE KINGDOM,
THE POWER, AND
THE GLORY

For thine is the kingdom, and the power,
and the glory, for ever. Amen.

MATTHEW 6:13

This "Model Prayer" that Jesus taught the disciples directs us to meditate on our relationship to God, the reverence due His wonderful name, the unfolding of His eternal kingdom, our submission to His will, His ability to provide our daily needs, His merciful forgiveness of sins, and His power to keep us from sin. Through contemplation of the marvelous attributes and abilities of God, our minds and hearts are moved to praise Him; and Jesus shows us how to do that one more time in the last phrase of this prayer.

"For thine is the kingdom." There is an old hymn of praise that begins, "I love Thy kingdom, Lord." The kingdom belongs to the King, and He rules supreme over everything and everyone in it. God's kingdom encompasses the patriarchs, prophets, priests, and saints of the Old Testament; the apostles, preachers, and missionaries of the New Testament; all born-again believers of the past, present, and future; the millennial kingdom; and the host of angels in heaven. And He has given us the key to His kingdom—salvation through Jesus Christ!

"And the power." It is the power of God that raised Jesus from the dead, supports His kingdom, and makes good on all His promises. He gives us the power to live the Christian life and to take us to heaven. The power of God through Jesus Christ has energized believers through the ages to do incredible things for Him.

"And the glory." No one has looked upon God in all His glory. But one day the whole earth shall behold Him in all his glory. "Thou art worthy, O Lord, to receive glory and honour and power: for thou hast created all things, and for thy pleasure they are and were created" (Revelation 4:11).

"Forever, Amen." Occasionally we hear the words of this remarkable prayer sung, and our hearts are filled with praise as they ring with the final thoughts—forever! How awesome to know that, "When we've been there ten thousand years, bright shining as the sun. We've no less days to sing His praise than when we first begun." And our hearts cry out, *Amen!*